Memoirs of Her Majesty's Prison Doctor

Memoirs of Her Majesty's Prison Doctor

Dr Gordon Cameron

Perseverance Books

MEMOIRS OF HER MAJESTY'S PRISON DOCTOR

Published by Perseverance Books

For information please email:
info@hmpdoctorsmemoirs.com

www.hmpdoctorsmemoirs.com

ISBN: 978-0-9570780-9-3

TABLE OF CONTENTS

FOREWORD

After working as a prison doctor in various prisons in the UK for over ten years, my head is so loaded with memories it is, metaphorically, on the point of exploding! I'm presented with two options – to keep everything to myself, taking my experiences and thoughts to the grave; or to purge my head of the prison material crammed in there by offloading them into print!

After pondering the matter for a while, I have chosen the latter option.

Even then, I have decided not only to be brief but also selective in reporting my experiences, for if I were to recount every single story, incident, happening that I have witnessed and/or observed over the period under consideration, it would require volumes upon volumes of paper for the task.

Aware that I am bound by the confidentiality of my profession, I will keep everything anonymous. I will refrain from using first names. Apart from providing a list of all the prisons I have so far worked in, I have intentionally avoided mentioning any prison by name when it comes to describing specific incidents, events, happenings, etc.

INTRODUCTION:
PRISON ROLL CALL

During my work as a prison doctor spanning a period of over a decade, I have treated every type of prisoner – from the most dangerous inmate kept in the Close Supervision Centre (CSC) of a Category A prison, to the relatively benign young drug addict imprisoned in a Young Offenders Institute (YOI) for committing petty crime to fund his/her addiction to drugs.

I have interacted with those placed high on the social ladder, from leading politicians, professionals, bank managers, right down to those on the lower end of the social ladder – drug addicts committing crime to fund their addiction.

I have met well-educated inmates – doctors, engineers, architects, etc. – as well as the barely educated, illiterates and semi-illiterates, among them Englishmen and women who are not only barely at home in 'Oxford English' but also have great difficulty writing even their names.

I have met individuals involved in some of the high profile cases that made headlines and filled the airwaves, such as a nurse jailed for deliberately injecting insulin into the IV-lines of his patients, or a father accused of deliberately setting a house ablaze, which in the end led to the death of several of his children.

I have, in other words, met the whole spectrum of prisoners in English prisons. I have met perpetrators of the most heinous crimes imaginable, for example the type involving the stabbing and beheading on the streets of London of an unarmed soldier going about his daily activities in civilian clothes. In contradistinction to these, I have, as I said earlier, met low key offenders, drug addicts, who engage in various kinds of crime to fund their addiction.

Barring the unexpected endeavours to set them free from their addiction to drugs, prison for such group of individuals becomes an aspect of the vicious cycle of their life – their craving for drugs, lack of resources to acquire drugs legally, engaging in crime with the goal to acquire the substances to which they are addicted, getting caught, sentenced, imprisoned, released, craving for drugs, committing crime, arrested and then back in prison – and so on and on and on it goes.

I have treated not only UK nationals, but a population group that could be considered as representing a mini-United Nations – nationals coming from countries ranging from Afghanistan to Ghana, even including the US.

I have treated the refined and cultured, among them a member of the House of Lords, the UK legislative Upper Chamber, as well as the rude and uncultured, individuals who have threatened me, who have been abusive to me, to the extent of telling me in the most crude terms to "f*** off!"

There are currently around 123 prisons in England and Wales. Over the period of ten years covered by this book, I have worked in about a third of them – 47 of them, to be precise.

I have worked in every category of prison, both male and female, as well as in every geographical location of the country – north, south, east and west.

Though not classified as a prison in the strictest sense, since they to a large extent bear the hallmark of a prison, I will – if only for the sake of this narrative – mention the Immigration Removal Centres as well.

Though I am yet to work in a prison in Scotland, I have spent one weekend working for the police in Aberdeen.

Below is the roll call of prisons, both female and male, where I have worked – arranged in alphabetical order.

Name	Location	County	Notes	Category
Altcourse	Liverpool	Merseyside		B
				C
Brinsford	Featherstone	Staffordshire	Young Offenders	HMYOI
Bristol	Horfield	Bristol		B
				A
Bullingdon	Arncott	Oxfordshire		B, C
Bure	Coltishall	Norfolk		C
Doncaster	Doncaster	South Yorkshire		B
Dovegate	Uttoxeter	Staffordshire		B
Durham	Durham	County Durham		B
Foston Hall	Foston	Derbyshire	Female Adults & Young Offenders	B
Frankland	Brasside	County Durham		A
Full Sutton	Full Sutton	East Riding of Yorkshire		A
Garth	Ulnes Watton	Lancashire		B
Hatfield	Hatfield Woodhouse	South Yorkshire		D
Hewell	Tardebigge	Worcestershire		B, C, D
Highpoint North	Sreadishall	Suffolk		C
Highpoint South	Stradishall	Suffolk		C
Hull	Kingston Upon Hull	East Riding of Yorkshire		B
Leeds	Leeds	West Yorkshire		B
Leicester	Leicester	Leicestershire		B
Leyhill	Torworth	Gloucestershire		D
Lincoln	Lincoln	Lincolnshire		B
Lindholme	Hatfield Woodhouse	South Yorkshire		C
Litlehey	Perry	Cambridgeshire		C
Long Lartin	South Littleton	Worcestershire		A

Name	Location	County	Notes	Category
Low Newton	Brasside	County Durham	Female Adults & Young Offenders	C
Lowdham Grange	Lowdahm	Nottinghamshire		B
Manchester	Manchester	Greater Manchester		A
Moorland	Hatfield	South Yorkshire		C
New Hall	Flocton	West Yorkshire	Female & Young Adults	C
Northumberland	Acklington	Northumberland		C
Norwich	Norwich	Norfolk		B, C
Oakwood	Featherstone	Staffordshire		C
				B, C
Peterborough	Peterborough	Cambridgeshire	Male Adults	B
Peterborough	Peterborough	Cambridgeshire	Female Adults	B
Preston	Preston	Lancashire		B
Ranby	Ranby	Nottinghamshire		C
Risley	Warrington	Cheshire		C
Rye Hill	Barby	Northamptonshire		B
Stocken	Stretton	Rutland		C
Stoke Heath	Stoke Heath	Shropshire	Young Offenders	
Sudbury	Sudbury	Derbyshire		D
Wakefield	Wakefield	West Yorkshire		A)
Wandsworth	Wandsworth	London		B
Wayland	Griston	Norfolk		C
Werrington	Werrington	Staffordshire	Young Offenders	
Wormwood Scrubs	Wormwood Scrubs	London		B
Wymott	Ulnes Walton	Lancashire		C

Concerning the Immigration Removal Centres (IRC), I have so far worked in two of them.

PART ONE
THE PRISON ESTABLISMENT

1) PRISON OR HOLIDAY CAMP?

During the 2011 riots in London which spread to various parts of the UK, the Prime Minister cut short his holiday overseas and returned to the country to lead the effort to curb the uprising and restore order.

"We shall hit back", he reassured the nation. "We shall punish those involved very hard!!"

Of course, I did not expect anything less of him.

As the head of government he had no choice but to portray himself as being able to restore "law and order". Indeed, he had no option but to be seen as a strong leader, capable of taking a tough stance, to give a firm impression of being able to restore law and order to the streets.

That was especially necessary considering that the London 2012 Olympic Games were only several months away.

"We shall punish the offenders hard!"

Well, for a section of the rioters, for those who had moved with the crowd, who had been carried away by the mob, who had been influenced by the momentum of the moment to commit crime, conviction could be a catastrophic experience, not only in regard to the custodial sentence it might lead to, but because of the even more damaging effect such a sentence might have for future job prospects. Persons thus affected would henceforth have to mention their conviction on their CV, which might well lead potential employers to deny them employment.

For a good proportion of those involved, I dare say the majority, those threats might be considered empty at best. To such group of individuals, sending them to prison, to a standard UK prison, would, in all likelihood, not be considered as punishment.

I dare indeed assert, at least based on the experience I gained interacting with them during my more than ten years' prison work, that some might have deliberately joined the mob with the aim of being arrested and sent back to jail. Indeed, for many serial offenders, individuals not used to any other form of existence than life behind the walls of a prison, a prison sentence does not necessarily mean punishment.

Prison for this group of individuals may well be regarded as a "holiday camp", a kind of sanctuary that offers them refuge from the hard realities of life in the community – a place where they do not need to care about earning money for food, rent, council tax, etc.

Not only that, it may also be perceived as a place with free access to reasonably well equipped gyms, free university education for those able and willing to pursue further studies, as well as a place where one could claim compensation, in some cases involving quite large sums of money, should something untoward happen to one – for example, should one slip, fall and sustain a fracture whilst exercising in the prison gym!

2) SCANDALOUS UK PRISONS

A little over four years after he had vowed to punish rioters on the streets of London by sending them to jail, the same Prime Minster, in a policy speech on February 8, 2016, promised an overhaul of the "scandalous British prison system".

Well, it may be scandalous in the way it is managed, for which I will present my own suggestions for improvement later on in my narration.

As far as the basic living conditions are concerned, they cannot, in my opinion, be described as scandalous, at least as compared to those pertaining to other parts of the world – not that I myself have toured any other prisons apart from those in the UK.

I've not arrived at this conclusion arbitrarily, for it's based on conversations I've had over the period I have worked in various UK prisons, with inmates, both British and foreigners, who had either served previous convictions in other prisons or who had been extradited from elsewhere to complete their various sentences in UK jails.

Whether they served their terms in Eastern Europe, Africa, Asia, South or Central America, the general consensus from them is that jail conditions in the UK are, if anything, too comfortable!

"These are not jails", one Polish national who claimed to have served prison terms both in his native Poland and Russia, told me. Over there, prisons are overcrowded – and one had to resort to bribing officers to get something to smoke.

A UK citizen, a diabetes patient, who was extradited from Panama to continue his sentence here, might very well confirm this. He told stories of overcrowded prisons and scarcity of food. According to him, he had to sleep on a blanket spread on a hard concrete floor. He went on to state that the insulin provided him was outdated.

Well, in spite of the poor quality of food provided over there, he got his blood sugar under control, regardless of whether his insulin was outdated or not. A paradoxical situation developed on his extradition to the UK to serve the rest of his term. Whereas he managed to keep his blood sugar under control in his previous jail with the outdated insulin supplied him, he struggled to do so with the best and up-to-date insulin given to him here. The reason was not difficult to fathom – in the British prison he could hardly resist the temptation to overeat the abundant supply of prison food!

3) PRIVATE VERSUS PUBLIC PRISONS

B efore I dwell further on my topic of prison conditions, I would like to give the reader a brief insight into the organisation of prisons in the UK.

There are two sets of prisons in the UK – those in the public sector and those in the private sector.

Public sector prisons in the UK are managed by Her Majesty's Prison Service (HMPS).

Private prisons are prisons that have been contracted out to private companies to be run on behalf of the Minister of Justice. The private companies involved in the running of such prisons are Sodexo Justice Services, Serco and G4S Justice Services.

All prisons in the UK, whether publicly or privately run, are inspected by Her Majesty's Inspectorate of Prisons.

My prison work has not been restricted to publicly run prisons. I have indeed worked in at least one prison managed by each of the above-named private companies.

4) PRISON CATEGORISATION

MALE PRISON/PRISONER CATEGORISATION: I will now consider the issue of prison categorisation: UK male prisons are classified into four categories: Categories A, B, C and D. The classification is based on the level of security in place in the establishment concerned – Cat A being the highest security level and Cat D the lowest.

Category A: Cat A prisons are used to house the most dangerous prisoners – those whose escape would be highly dangerous to the public or national security. To prevent this from happening, a high level of security is in place in such establishments.

Perhaps you, the reader, can recall high profile cases involving rape, murder, terrorism, etc., that have made headlines – publicised by Radio, TV, the Print media, etc., in the recent past? Those involved are likely serving their terms in a Cat A prison as you read through these lines.

Category B: Cat B prisons house inmates who do not require maximum security, and yet require a high level of security to prevent them from escaping into the community.

Even without referring to any official prison statistics, based on my own experience, Cat B prisons constitute the majority of prisons in the UK. They usually also serve as remand prisons. For the sake of readers not familiar with the term "remand prisons" or "remand prisoners", I shall pause to provide a short explanation.

Remand prisoners are those detained in prison pending their trial. They have usually not been convicted of a criminal offence and are awaiting trials following a not guilty plea.

Apart from the highly dangerous prisoners who are remanded in Cat A prisons, prisoners on remand are usually sent to Cat B prisons.

As a result of their remand status, there is quite a high turnover of prisoners in Cat B prisons. One could compare them to a hospital ward where emergency cases are first admitted and later distributed to various wards of the hospital concerned or transferred to other specialist centres.

Though this is not backed by any study, from my own point of view, due to its remand status, the Cat B prison is the most challenging environment for the healthcare staff. It could probably be said for prison staff in general. As I have reiterated on several occasions, I would like as far as possible to restrict myself to healthcare.

As a result of its remand status, the Category B prison usually houses quite a high number of drug addicts and alcoholics awaiting sentencing. Not only do such persons arrive in prison displaying various stages of drug withdrawal, during their stay they pose a challenge to healthcare due to their addiction.

I will return to the issue later on in my narration when I come to deal with the problem of drug abuse in prisons.

Category C: Cat C prisons are home to inmates who cannot be trusted in open prison conditions, but will not necessarily have the intention, the will or the determination, to make any real attempt of escape from the prison.

Category D: Cat D prisons are home to inmates who can be reasonably trusted not to try to escape.

Category A, B and C prisons are called *closed* prisons, whereas, Cat D prisons are called *open* prisons.

Usually prisoners spend the initial stages of their sentences in Cat A and B prisons. On fulfilment of some laid down criteria, they are moved to Cat C prisons midway through their sentence and Cat D prisons towards the end of their sentence.

YOI (Young Offenders Institute) are home to offenders between the ages of 18 and 21 years.

This leads me to the case of a young man who recognised me as I worked at the Reception of a Cat B prison.

"Do you remember me, sir?"

"Not exactly, do remind me."

"I attended your clinic in a YOI?"

"What are you doing here?"

"Well, I have turned 21, so I have been moved into an adult prison."

"I wish you all the best for your future, young man."

"Thank you, sir!"

How I wished the prison service would exercise some degree of flexibility in such matters!

Indeed if I had my own way, I would allow such inmates who had already begun their sentence at the YOI, provided they did not have a considerable number of years left to serve, to serve their remaining sentence at the YOI. It is only after they have re-offended, after their release, that they should be sent to the adult prison. In my opinion, moving them from the YOI to the adult prison just because they have turned 21 is not an optimal solution. Indeed moving them from the fairly well protected environment of the YOI to a standard Cat B prison housing adult criminals, is tantamount to taking a jump from the frying pan into the fire!

***

Not only are the prisons categorised into four groups, the prisoners are also accordingly categorized into Cat A, B, C or D prisoners based on the severity of their respective crime and the risk they might pose to the public were they ever to escape.

Category A (Cat A) Prisoners: As I indicated above, Cat A prisoners are the most dangerous. Their crimes may involve murder, rape, armed robbery, firearms offences, possession of or supplying explosives, terrorism, etc.

Category A prisoners on their part are further divided into Standard Risk, High Risk, and Exceptional Risk prisoners, based on their likelihood of escaping.

Category B (Cat B) Prisoners: These are prisoners who do not require maximum security, and yet require a high level of security to prevent them from escaping into the community.

Category C (Cat C) Prisoners: Inmates who were initially classified as Cat B are reclassified as Cat C when they are deemed not to necessarily have the intention, the will or the determination to make any real attempt to escape from the prison.

Category D (Cat D) Prisoners: Prisoners approaching the end of their prison terms and who can be reasonably trusted not to attempt to escape are classified as Cat D prisoners. They may be issued a Release On Temporary Licence (ROTL) to work in the community or to go on "home leave". This is aimed at offering them the opportunity to gradually prepare for a permanent return to life in the community.

FEMALE PRISON/PRISONER CATEGORISATION: Classification of female prisons and prisoners is based on the principles outlined above for their male counterparts; the only difference lies in terminology.
Below are the terminologies used for female prisons/prisoners with their corresponding male equivalents.

Female Restricted – Male Cat A
Female Closed – Male Cat B
Female Semi-Open – Male Cat C
Female Open – Male Class D

RECATEGORISATION: After a while a Class A prisoner who fulfils some laid down conditions, may be recategorised as Class B.
A Cat B prisoner on his part may gain Cat C status whereas a Cat C prisoner may be recategorised as a Cat D prisoner.

The reverse situation also applies. An inmate of the lower category, who abuses his/her privilege could be recategorised into a higher risk category.

I used to work in a Cat C prison that was neighbour to a Cat D prison. Initially both were administered separately. In the course of time, both were brought under the same administration.

Occasionally, some of the residents were sent from the closed Cat C prison to the open Cat D prison only to be sent back again. If one asked them what happened, these were some of their answers:

"I failed a drug test."

"I returned late from a *home leave*."

"I have been accused of trading my prescription drugs."

A MIXTURE OF VARIOUS CATEGORIES: Prisoners of various categories may be housed in the same prison. For example one might meet Cat B prisoners in a Cat A prison – the majority of inmates would however be Cat A prisoners.

I do not wish to go into a detailed discussion of why this is the case. Suffice to say that it is the category of the prisoner that is the determining factor. For example, a Cat B prisoner in Cat A prison is subjected to fewer restrictions compared to inmates in the Cat A category.

5) SPECIAL PRISON WINGS

Having dealt with the prison categorisation in general, I shall now mention two special wings of the prison, namely the Segregation and Vulnerable Prisoners Wings.

SEGREGATION WING: A PRISON WITHIN A PRISON

The Segregation Unit – known in other prisons as the Care and Separation Unit (CSU) or Inmates Recovery Unit (IRU) can be described as a "prison within a prison".

Prisoners are kept in the Segregation Unit for various reasons.

Those who commit offences such as assaulting other inmates, or setting fire to their cells; those who abuse, assault or attempt to assault staff – the governor, prison officers, healthcare staff, etc.

Not only those who cause harm to others are sent to the Segregation Wing. Instead some inmates are kept in segregation for their own protection.

In one prison I entered, I was surprised by the large number of inmates being kept in the Segregation Wing, so I decided to find out from one of the officers.

"Well, quite a good proportion of them have applied to be sent here for their own protection", was his reply.

"What do you mean by that?" I wanted to know.

"Well, some are indebted to other prisoners and are not in a position to pay their debts. In such a situation, they apply to be sent here for their own protection!"

"How do they get themselves into debt in the first place?"

"Your guess is as good as mine, doc!"

"Drugs?"

"Indeed!"

As far as matters relating to their health is concerned, it is usually required that inmates in the Segregation Unit are seen by the doctor on every other day. In the majority of prisons where I worked, the doctor's segregation rounds usually take place on Mondays, Wednesdays and Fridays; in a few cases they are held on Tuesdays, Thursdays and Saturdays.

Prisons go to great lengths to meet the laid-down requirement in regard to the routine three-time weekly GP visits. Is it because of the need to appear in a good light in matters of prison inspection? Indeed, there have been several instances when I have been booked to work in a prison on a bank holiday with the sole purpose of conducting segregation rounds. The prisons involved would not only pay for my mileage – in some cases involving a total of 100 miles or more – but also pay me for a whole session's work (four hours) for a job that might take a mere half an hour to complete.

Segregation inmates who happen to be on medication have them dispensed by a nurse who goes specially to do so one, two or three times daily as the case may be. Later on in my narration, I will touch on the issue of supervised and unsupervised medication dispensing in the prison setting. Patients in the Segregation Wing are not permitted to keep their medication even if they were allowed to do so prior to their transfer.

THE VULNERABLE PRISONERS UNIT

In the above section, I spoke about the Segregation Unit. Another unit is the Vulnerable Prisoner (VP) Unit.

It is a prison wing where inmates who are deemed at risk of being subjected to bullying, harassment, assault, etc., from the mainstream prison population are kept for their own protection.

Inmates in the VP wing are likely to be sex offenders. There are few prisons in the UK that houses exclusively sex offenders. I visited one in the south east, which lies in such a remote and isolated place that I had difficulty locating it, even with the help of my Sat Nav.

Those sex offenders who end up in a normal Cat B or Cat A prison are usually kept in the VP (Vulnerable Prisoners) Wing for their own protection. This is because sex offenders tend to be looked upon with scorn by the mainstream prison population. For their own protection, therefore, they are either sent to a prison housing exclusively sex offenders or, if that is not possible, they are sent to the Vulnerable Prisoners' Wing of the prison.

Apart from this group of people, police informers, ex-police officers and magistrates may be kept in the Vulnerable Prisoners Unit.

Prisoners who do not belong to the above category, but who are involved in high profile cases, indeed whose cases have generated public interest, may also be kept in the VP Wing for their own protection.

Inmates in the Vulnerable Prisoners Unit are generally not allowed to interact with the mainstream prison population. In the issue of healthcare, they are usually allocated a special clinic day. If it happens for example to be a Tuesday, only VP patients are given a routine doctor's appointment on that day.

Should the condition of a mainstream prisoner require that he or she be seen on the day allocated for VP prisoners, they are seen either before the VPs or after them.

The reverse is also true – vulnerable prisoners who need medical attention outside the day allocated for them will be seen either before or after the mainstream prisoners. As they wait to be seen, they are kept in special holding units/cells out of sight of the mainstream prisoners.

6) MY OWN CLASSIFICATION OF PRISONERS

Based on my several years' experience working as a prison doctor, I have come up with my own classification of prison inmates based on the type of offence for which they have been convicted. I must stress that this classification is not scientifically based, but is subjective, based purely on my own experience.

Sex offenders

Under this category are inmates convicted of rape, paedophilia, online pornography, indecent assault, etc.

The ages of inmates may range from early twenties far into the eighties.

Based on my own observation, those aged up to around 40 years are serving terms for rape. If they happen to be beyond 40 years old, they might have been sentenced at an earlier age.

Those sex offenders sentenced for the first time at an advanced age are likely to be in prison for paedophilia, or child pornography-related offences, or both.

A fact that struck me in my conversation with those serving various terms for rape is the fact that hardly any of them admitted to forcibly sleeping with their accusers. Instead the majority of them claimed they had been framed by their accusers after consensual sex.

I still remember the case of a young man of about 28 years who told me he was operating a one-man delivery service in his own company. He went on to narrate the fact that he was literally pursued by a young lady who happened to live in an area where he used to deliver goods on a regular basis. Eventually he gave in to her approaches. In the process, he concealed the fact that he was married, and that he was making plans for his wife in Africa to join him in the UK. He went on to state that it came to a point when his new-found lover demanded that he marry her – and in the end she found out that he was in fact married to a woman in Africa. She demanded that he end his relationship with the African lady, something he was not prepared to do.

One day he was at home when he heard knocking on his door. Unsuspecting, he opened the door only to be met by two police officers. They made known to him the reason of their coming – he had been accused of rape!

Eventually, the matter came to court. He did not deny that he had had an affair with his accuser, but he insisted it was consensual.

In the end the jury believed and favoured the case of the prosecution. At the time of our meeting the accused had just started a seven-year prison term for rape. His imprisonment had led not only to the collapse of his business, but also to the loss of his home. He was so convinced of his innocence, however, that when his appeal was rejected, he decided to take his case to the European Court of Human Rights.

I do not know what became of the matter, for after a while I stopped going to work in the prison where he was serving his sentence. I must emphasise that I am just reproducing one side of the story.

Terrorism related

Prisoners on remand for or convicted of terrorism-related offences are usually sent to Category A prisons.

I have treated individuals involved in some of the most high profile terrorism-related cases of the recent past; these include those linked with the July 7, 2005 bombing of the London Underground as well as the pair who carried out the daylight assassination of a serving soldier on the streets of London.

Murder and manslaughter

I have met and treated a sizeable number of those who have taken the lives of others. I still have in mind a young man sentenced for manslaughter. Employed as an orderly or "bouncer" for a disco, he was engaged in a tussle with a group he was preventing from entering the disco. In the process he delivered a blow to one of them that sent the man crashing to the floor. In the process the man's head hit the hard floor and he went into a coma never to regain consciousness.

Drug related offenders

I have sub-classified this group of offenders into three:
1) the pure drug dealers
2) the dealer plus consumer
3) the pure consumers

The pure drug dealers are serving terms for dealing in drugs. They might have had various roles in the supply chain.

They might be UK citizens who have travelled to the supply source in Africa, Asia, South America, etc., to collect drugs from local agents. In the process they might have been arrested in the source country or they might have managed to escape arrest in the source country only to be arrested at their various points of entry in the UK. Those UK nationals arrested in foreign lands might initially have been jailed in the countries concerned and extradited later to serve the remainder of their sentences in the UK.

Some foreign nationals might also be arrested trying to smuggle such substances into the country, as in the case of an elderly African lady, just shy of her 60th birthday at the time of our meeting, who was arrested trying to smuggle drugs from Holland into the UK.

I also have in mind an attractive young lady, aged about 25, the type many a gentleman may be inclined to fall in love with on the first meeting. Not only did she boast good looks, she appeared to be intelligent and also a gifted speaker. As if that were not enough, she happened to bear the alias "Pinky!" After she had left the consulting room I turned to the nurse chaperoning me.

"An awesome young lady; what brought her to prison?"

"I have no idea; wait a moment, I'll go and check from the Prison Service computer in the adjacent room." (Prison Health Care and Prison Service have different computer systems with different databases.) She returned a few minutes later. "She has been sentenced for drug-related offences. She served as a go-between, for an international drug ring and their UK distributers."

"A very charming lady! If the drug ring wanted to work with someone who would fall under the least suspicion, they had no doubt found in her the right candidate."

When it comes to drug smuggling, my experience is that hardly any would want to admit their direct involvement – as in the case of a young inmate from West Africa. According to his account he used to be a worker at Heathrow. At the time of his arrest he was no longer working there. His contact in Africa asked him to meet someone arriving in the UK. Since he himself was no longer working at Heathrow, he begged another acquaintance who was working there to meet the person. She collected the item and kept it in her locker. She brought it to his house when he was back from work. The traveller from West Africa had in the meantime come to his house to pick up the item. Just about that time, the police arrived to arrest them both. " Doc, I was not aware; never aware of the contents of the package." he insisted.

Then there was the case of an elderly 62-year-old Englishman extradited from Brazil to serve the remainder of his sentence in the UK. According to him he had set up a business in the Gambia. His wife remained in the UK, visiting him occasionally. In the course of his stay in the Gambia, he got to know a man from Nigeria and in due course they became close friends. One day his Nigerian friend said to him: "I'd like to send you on a mission to Brazil to collect something valuable for me." Initially he was not keen to go. In the end however he agreed to go.

As it turned out, it was cocaine. He was arrested, tried and imprisoned in Brazil. After serving three and half years of his sentence in Brazil he was extradited to the UK to serve the rest of his sentence. He also maintained he was not aware of the contents of the parcel!

As in the cases of all extradited back to the UK to complete a sentence, he was delighted to be able to put the "hell" of prison life in Brazil behind him, preferring the relatively comfortable conditions of prison life in the UK.

One inmate who was nearing the end of his sentence for importing large amounts of drugs into the UK was unrepentant. "So long as there is demand there will be supply!" he stated unequivocally. That was his job – a job that had enabled him to give his children a good education, to help them rise above the low social class he was born into so they did not have to resort to what he was engaged in to support them and their children!

He had already served various prison terms as a result of drug-dealing activities. He could not guarantee that he wouldn't return to prison again on his release!

Before I turn my attention from this group I would like to mention those who intentionally commit crime to get the opportunity to go to prison to deal in drugs! I could not imagine anyone favouring this recourse until one day an officer who was escorting me to the gate after my duty in one prison enlightened me.

"Doc, do you see that guy ahead of us being escorted by the officer?"

"Yes, I do. What's the matter with him?"

"He is a well-known drug dealer in the city."

"Indeed?!"

"We suspect him of intentionally committing his crime in order to get the opportunity to expand his drug trade in prison!"

"So what did he do?"

"He is on remand for child molesting. It is said that he gave his son a violent whack in a public place. It is believed he did so intentionally. His real motive was to get the opportunity to be in prison, to supervise his drug trade here."

"That's an extraordinary accusation!"

"It's an open secret, but our hands are bound. The law must be allowed to take its course. He is a child abuser, so he must be sent to jail – notwithstanding his ulterior motives."

The next group is comprised of the dealer-addicts. They are those who deal in drugs to fund their own addiction. They may be in prison, either for being caught in the possession of drugs – usually not large amounts – or for committing crime to earn additional money to spend on drugs.

Finally, I come to the ***"pure druggies or junkies"*** – those who commit crime to fund their addiction. For the sake of this discussion,

I will also include those sentenced for committing thefts to fund their alcohol addiction. (I will return to this group of prisoners at a later stage.)

One usually meets them in Cat B/Remand Prisons, and in most cases they are not serving a prison sentence for the first time. Hardly anyone of them regards a prison sentence as a form of punishment. Instead, a good proportion, if not the overwhelming majority, will admit that, as far as they are concerned, prison is a kind of home, a community they are happy to be a part of.

During reception screening, these are some of the statements that may issue from their lips.

"Doc, I'm looking forward to the prison's warm meals; it will be the first I am privileged to enjoy for some time."

"I was living rough on the street and am happy to be back."

"I was hungry so shoplifted some food from the supermarket. You call that a crime, Doc?"

Some arrive in prison very unkempt; with no fixed abode, they might not have had a shower and/or changed their clothing for days, if not weeks or even months!

Some sink into deep depression towards the end of their sentences; indeed, the prospect of them being sent back into the community could lead to sleepless nights for many a "druggy".

Miscellaneous

Under this group I shall include all prison inmates not classified into any of the aforementioned groups. They may be in prison for offences such as non-payment of fines, non-payment of council tax, death by dangerous driving, DWD (driving while disqualified,), drink driving, ABH (actual bodily harm), GBH (grievous bodily harm) etc.

7) THOSE WHO CALL PRISON *HOME!*

I t did not take long for me to work in prison to become aware of one group of inmates – namely frequent returnees to prison. This group of prisoners falls into two categories – the *institutionalised prisoners* and prisoners with various addiction problems.

INSTITUTIONALISED PRISONERS: Some inmates have become so used to prison life that they can hardly cope with the normal routine of life in freedom. Such prisoners, the institutional prisoners, on their release from prison deliberately commit crime so as to be sent back *home*.

Collins, my favourite prison officer in a prison where I worked for a considerable period of time, narrated a case of an inmate who held the personal record he was keeping of re-offenders. It involved an inmate who left the gates of a prison at 9am only to return at 5pm the same day. What happened? On reaching the community, he walked straight into the next available shop and blatantly committed a shoplifting offence.

That record was broken by an inmate of a female prison a few years after Collins had told me of the first case. The lady involved had no need to travel far into the community on her release to commit her crime. Instead she headed straight for the prison staff car park a short distance from the main prison gate. She picked up a sharp object she found on the pavement and with it brazenly targeted scores of cars parked there, inflicting long deep scratches in the paintwork, causing thousands of pounds' worth of damage. As might be expected, she was immediately re-arrested and remanded in the same prison!

In the end she ended up on the Segregation Wing. When I made my usual afternoon rounds that day, her loud yells could be heard everywhere on the wing. It was when I inquired about the reason behind her agitation that I was told the story I have just narrated.

Later on, I learnt from one of the nursing staff that the inmate in question had been overheard threatening to murder someone in order to gain a long prison sentence!

Then there's the case of a young man I met at a young offenders' institute. He told me he first came into conflict with the law at the age of 13 years and had since then been going in and out of prison. At the time of our meeting he was 19. He went on to state that his alcoholic mother had passed away when he was quite young. He told me his father, also an alcoholic, had introduced him to alcohol at an early age. At the time of our meeting his father was serving a life sentence for murder.

As an only child, he had no other relative in the free world. He told me, without any indication of regret or remorse in his face, that he preferred life in prison to life outside. He just could not cope outside, he admitted.

The occurrence of short-term returnees increases in winter for obvious reasons – the inclement weather. "I have been sleeping very rough since my release from prison a few weeks ago", one inmate confided in me. "At least now I have a roof over my head and I don't have to freeze." He added: "Apart from that there's the free prison food!"

"DRUGGIES": Apart from the institutionalised prisoners, another group of prisoners who frequently return to prison are those with addiction problems – I touched on the group in the previous chapter. They may be addicted to one or more of the substances of addiction – alcohol, heroin, cocaine, cannabis, diazepam, etc.

Whereas individuals classified as institutionalised prisoners deliberately commit crime to gain access to prison, drug addicts may not necessarily harbour that intention. Instead, they may be forced to commit crime – theft, burglary, fraud, etc., to acquire the funds needed to purchase the substance they are addicted to. They may indeed wish they could stay out of crime as illustrated by the following entry in the record of a patient soon to be released:

"She has spent the majority of her adult life in prison and is very anxious in relation to her release and possible drug use. She wishes to 'lead a normal life' and does not wish to return to prison. Although she states she has every intention of staying clean, she is aware that in the past she has resorted to drug-seeking behaviours when placed under pressures mentally. She has requested an increase in her Methadone to enable her to remain stable when released – agreed increase of Methadone 10ml to 40ml; discussed issues around tolerance levels and harm reduction should she be tempted to use drugs on release; made aware of dangers."

The following conversation ensued between myself and an inmate due for release in a few days' time:

"You are surely happy your time in jail is over!"

"Of course, I want to get out of here."

"How long did you serve?"

"I was sentenced to 12 weeks – reduced to six."

"What for?"

"Shoplifting. I needed the cash for 'gear' [heroin]."

"I wish you all the best for your life"

"Thanks."

"This is surely going to be your last time in jail, isn't it?"

"For sure, doc! I'm getting older and older. It's about time I sorted out my life."

"Promise?"

"You have my word!"

The saying has it that the spirit is willing but the flesh is weak. It took only a couple of weeks before he was sent back to prison. I was the doctor on reception duty that evening. He had to see me to get a prescription for methadone.

"You are back again! What happened?"

"You remember I promised you never to come back? Initially I did my best, doc, to stay clean of drugs. Unfortunately, in the end I could not resist the temptation to return to them. That got me into trouble. I was caught shoplifting – I needed money for gear!"

"What items did you shoplift?"

"Aftershave and men's cologne."

8) UNITED NATION OF PRISONERS

Partly as a result of its historical links to various parts of the world, the UK is home to a good proportion of natives of its former colonies. Besides that it also boasts quite a sizable population of citizens from other European countries as well as citizens from the rest of the world outside of the Commonwealth.

How does the prison population reflect that of the general population?

The other day I read a passage from a book written by a Nigerian pastor based in London. He drew attention to the fact that there is a disproportionately higher number of blacks languishing in UK jails, as compared to the general population.

As I said earlier, I do not want to resort to any statistics in my narration. I also do not wish to dispute studies that have concluded that, based on the overall population make-up of the UK, blacks are over represented in UK jails. The fact of those statistics was not immediately obvious to me as I moved around the country working in one prison after the other.

Certainly, there are quite a good number of blacks in London prisons – but should that come as a surprise to anyone? Indeed, these days when I happen to be walking on the streets of parts of London, in particular the north and east, I begin to ask myself whether I, indeed, find myself on the streets of the British capital. Indeed, sometimes I feel I could be in Lagos, Nigeria; or in Accra, Ghana, or perhaps in Kingston Jamaica when strolling along some parts of London. It is not surprising that some, these days, consider London not as part of the UK, but instead as the centre of a much wider worldwide community. I personally tend to regard London as the Commonwealth capital rather than the British capital.

Should it then come as a surprise that blacks in particular and BAME[1] in general are quite well represented in London prisons?

Even in the case of London, apart from the statistics, when I worked as a doctor in a couple of prisons there I did not have the feeling that blacks were over represented. Instead the impression I gained was that of a prison population akin to a gathering of a mini United Nations.

Indeed, from each corner of the globe – from the US, to New Zealand, right through to Pakistan, Chile and Brazil – every population group of the planet could be found.

Not only could one be confronted with individuals of various ethnic backgrounds, one could also come across individuals who came into being by way of the most unlikely genetic combinations of humanity imaginable.

For example, one inmate told me he was the product of a relationship between a Turkish lady and a gentleman from Ghana! Another inmate told me he had a Pakistani father and a Thai mother. Then there was the case of a jovial young man who told me he had Jewish, Jamaican, English – and if my memory serves me right – Iranian ancestry! Pardon me, dear reader, if I no longer remember the exact ethnic combination of his grandparents! As far as I recall, his mother was the product of a relationship between a Jewish lady and a Jamaican man. His father on his part boasted an English mother and an Iranian father.

"So what do you think I am?" he asked jovially.

"A child of God!" was my reply.

"Sometime I can hardly control my emotions", he confessed. "At times they are up, at other times down; sometimes I feel restless. Doc, do you think it is the result of this weird combination of blood flowing through my veins?"

"No idea!"

"But you are a doctor!"

"Well, doctors are not there to solve all medical problems!"

---

[1]   Abbreviation: British. Black, Asian, and minority ethnic (used to refer to members of non-white communities in the UK).

As one moves away from London and heads northwards avoiding prisons in major cities like Birmingham and Manchester and heads towards prisons such as those in Durham, Sutton and Hull, the prison population becomes overwhelmingly white British.

The same applies to the population make-up of prisons in Norwich to the southeast and Bristol to the southwest of the British capital.

9) DAILY PRISONER ROUTINE

I do not want to go into details concerning the daily routine of prison life. For the sake of this narration, I shall give a quick overview of life in a UK prison based on my experience.

It can be divided into morning, afternoon and night. As far as a GP is concerned, the night is of little relevance. Nurses are usually there around the clock. In the case of GPs, prisons usually resort to the doctor on-call service to cover night cases.

The day begins with the morning roll call followed by breakfast.

Inmates are then moved around to various departments – healthcare, works, education, etc.

Lunch is around noon, followed by a period of rest (lockdown).

Around 2pm prisoners are "unlocked" for the afternoon movement. Just as in the case of the morning, they may be moved to various departments – healthcare, education, workshop, the gym to engage in various activities.

The evening meal is around 5:30pm, followed by the evening roll call. The final lockdown for the night is usually around 6:30pm.

10) IRRITATION WITH A FEMALE PRISON OFFICER'S THOROUGH SEARCH!

F or obvious reasons, security at the gate of a prison is tight – tightest at Cat A prisons and less so in Cat D prisons.

On arrival at the security gate, one is required to produce a form of photo ID. What is usually accepted is either a passport or a driving licence.

Usually, by the time one turns up at the gate, the department one is visiting, in my case the healthcare department, should have applied and received a gate pass. If that is the case, the matter becomes simple – one's name would already have been submitted to the gate. The officers only need to verify or cross-check with one's photo ID. After they have verified one's identity, they will call the department to request one of them to come to the gate to receive the visitor.

On some occasions, the department fails or forgets to submit the paperwork at the gate. This could delay matters considerably. After consulting with the team leader, the gate may allow one to go through without the paperwork. It is a matter of discretion. Some may insist that the department completes the paperwork and submits it at the gate before one is allowed to proceed further.

Before one is allowed to proceed any further after the identity check, most prisons present the visitor with a sheet listing items one is not permitted to carry into the prison. One has to read through the list and sign to declare one is not carrying any of the items listed in his bag or on him as the case may be.

Apart from items that one would consider reasonable as not being allowed in the prison – mobile phones, recording devices, weapons, other sharp items such as knives, pairs of scissors, razors, etc. – I was surprised to find chewing gum listed as one of the forbidden items. I beg the reader's pardon for no longer recalling exactly the explanation I was offered when I inquired about the reason behind the banning of chewing gum from the prison. The only thing I recall is that it poses a security risk, but exactly what kind of security risk it poses is not clear to me.

After one has signed the sheet the usual practice is for security to issue a temporarily visitor's badge/ID on a lanyard neck strap, which one hangs around the neck like a necklace. Some prisons issue a temporarily visitor's ID or name badge which can be fastened to one's clothes with a pin or curved safety pin.

Some prisons go a step further and take photographs of visitors to produce on-the-spot photo IDs.

I thought the IDs listed above were the only types of visitors' IDs and name badges until I was booked into a Cat B prison run by one of the private companies I mentioned earlier. For reasons best known to themselves, this particular prison has opted for wristbands, like the type used to identify new-born babies on the maternity ward!

I was really surprised when on the very first day I went to work there, after I had gone through a rigid gate check, the officer at the gate pulled a wristband from a drawer and began to tie it around my wrist.

"Miss, what's that for?" I inquired, taken aback.

"Well, that is our visitor's badge!"

"I have been to several prisons. No prison does it this way; usually it is something to hang around the neck or affix to the pocket of the coat or shirt."

"Well, this is what we do here! You are required to keep it on you throughout your time here and hand it back to security on your departure." I felt quite awkward wearing it.

When I started working in prison in 2005, the biometric system of identification had not been introduced at the prison gate. In those days, I worked mostly in Cat B and C prisons. After my ID had been checked and my bag searched, I was usually permitted to proceed into the waiting room to take a seat until someone came to pick me up.

As I write this account in 2016, biometric screening has become the norm in almost every prison I visit, with the exception of the open prisons.

These days when I turn up at the gate of a prison I have been booked to work in for the first time, the first thing that usually happen is the taking of my biometrics, never mind whether that day is likely to be the first and last time I would be there.

After I have identified myself, I am summoned to the biometric device.

"Please place your ring, middle and index fingers on the system."

"Which hand please?"

"Never mind which."

Without any further comment, I oblige.

After the officer has occupied himself with the computer screening for a while, the order comes for me to remove my fingers. The thought that I had put the "ordeal" behind me turns out to be premature.

"Please do so with the other hand!"

"My goodness", I murmur to myself, "am I a doctor going to do my best to save lives or a suspected criminal!"

Well, there is no time to argue ... any challenge and I could be shown to the gate of the prison door. Since I needed the "Queen's head", as my friend has Christened the British pound, I had to keep quiet.

As if the "ordeal" I have just described were not enough, the officer would then turn to me and say: "We need your photo as well. You need to go backwards and step in the square marked on the floor to be in the focus of the camera."

"Where please?"

"A few metres behind you, please."

I take a few steps backward and step into the area described.

"Go back a bit, sir."

I do as required.

"Look straight into the camera, sir!"

I obey.

"Please smile a little!"

There's a click and a flash! My picture is taken.

Moments later I'm handed a visitor's pass bearing my photo that I am required to hang around my neck throughout the time I spend in the prison that day.

That is not the end of the security screening, mind you. The next stage is the searching.

Usually a male visitor is searched by a male officer. That is not always the case however. In a few cases, probably due to a shortage of male staff on the day in question, I have been searched by a female officer. On one occasion I was searched by a young female officer, barely 19 years of age.

Whether it was because of insecurity on her part, or due to an excess of ambition on her part, I found her search went beyond what I was usually used to. It came to a point when I was tempted to disobey her instructions and instead demand that I speak to her superior. In the end I decided not to escalate the matter and allowed things to take its course.

After "passing" the security "test", one has to wait to be collected, which usually takes a few minutes. On one occasion, however, I had to wait almost an hour! Initially, I used to complain. Later I took the advice of another doctor who started working in the prison prior to me.

"Why are you concerned, friend? They pay you from the very moment you arrive, don't they?"

"But that is a waste of time and money!"

"Well, I used to think just like you but no longer care. After all, what does it matter?"

Eventually, someone from the department one is assigned to work in for the day – in my case a nurse or healthcare person – turns up to fetch and escort one to the place of work.

At the end of the day's assignment one is escorted right down to the security gate. The principle is that any visitor who does not draw keys is not permitted to move around the premises of the prison unescorted.

There are times when one has finished one's duty, when there is no one going to the gate. In this case, the nonchalant point of view of my doctor friend does not hold sway, for once one's timesheet has been signed (and that is usually the case before one is escorted out of the gate), any time spent in the prison will not be paid.

11) "LOCK IT! PROVE IT!"

K eys and locks abound in the prison. It is required that every door or gate in the prison is locked at all times. "Lock it! Prove it!" is a metal-plated inscription installed near the locking mechanism of almost every prison door or gate.

It took me quite a while to be handed keys. Two factors contributed to this. Initially, I was not a regular visitor at any of the prisons – instead I was sent there only sporadically. Secondly, I was not employed directly by the prison, but went there as an agency doctor.

Without access to one's own keys one is completely at the mercy of others. The doctors' room would be locked on my arrival. My escort unlocks it and grants me access. If I have to leave it for any reason, I have to get someone to lock it immediately after me.

The embarrassing aspect of not being in possession of keys is that when one has the need to use the toilet, one has to look around for someone to open the door.

First a key holder locks the door to the doctors' room and then leads me to the toilet. After he/she has unlocked it to grant me entry/access, the individual will hang around until I have finished my "business" to lock up the toilet and accompany me to the doctors' room to unlock it. It is not always that straightforward. It may well be the case that, at the very moment when one has to use the toilet, there is no staff member around.

Even after one has been let into the toilet, getting out after one has completed one's business might not be without problems.

One day after I had been let into the toilet, the staff member who let me in could not wait for me to finish as he had to leave me to attend to an urgent call.

"Doc, I will leave the corridor door open. When you get out, please find someone to lock it up!"

Not long after he was gone, just as I was still on the toilet, an officer who was passing by, noticing the lock to the corridor door I just referred to was unlocked, acted instinctively in line with the general prison rule – "lock it and secure it!" – and he locked it!

After I had finished my "business", I stepped out of the toilet room only to discover I was trapped by locked doors! What was to be done? Well, I had no choice other than to bang loudly on the door. Fortunately, the noise was soon heard and someone came to my rescue.

Once I had an unpleasant birthday present. I had indeed resolved not to work on that special occasion; but then on the day before the occasion, I received a call from my agency. A prison was desperately in need of cover on that day – would I be available for help? I really wished I could turn down the offer, but no, pressing financial needs compelled me to accept it.

The day passed without any incident. My session was to end at 4pm. A few minutes before that time, a nurse entered the room with a shortlist of prescriptions that needed to be filled. After handing the list over she left the room. My thinking was that she would be in the staff room.

It took me about ten minutes to get the job done. When I stepped outside my room, there was an eerie silence along the corridor.

"Hello, is someone there?"

No response.

"Hello, there! Please get me out of here!"

Still no response...

"Hello, hello!" I called out louder.

After a while I noticed several metres away an officer escorting prisoners along the corridors of the prison.

"Hello, hello, hello!" I cried out at the top of my voice.

Fortunately he heard my cry for help and came to my rescue.

The officer could only wonder – how on earth had they left me alone!!

He was going to ensure the matter was investigated for indeed it is against security protocol to leave a visitor without a key in that manner.

What a birthday present that was!!

That was not the first time I had been in that awkward situation. I had experienced a similar situation about two years earlier in another prison. I was in the doctors' room doing administrative work – writing prescriptions, reading through patient reports, writing referral letters, etc. To give me the needed quiet, I shut the door to the room.

All along, I thought there were other staff members in the staff room. At the end of my session at 5pm, I opened the door to realise that everyone had left! The doctor's office happened to be situated above a unit that served as a kind of hospital ward (more on hospital-like wards in prisons later) which was staffed around the clock. There were staff there I could have rung for help. I could also have rung the gate to make them aware of my predicament. But I had a problem – the telephone in the doctors' room was out of service. Under the circumstances, I saw no other option but to press the emergency buzzer (more on the emergency buzzer later)!

I knew what would happen in response to that – a host of prison officers rushing in from all directions in response to the alarm.

And that's what happened! Barely a minute lapsed before I heard the sound of footsteps hurrying in the direction of my room. I got out of the room and into the corridor to calm them down. They certainly were not amused! Under the circumstances, however, I think they understood my action.

On one occasion, one officer of the gate, who had seen me come and go for months and probably thinking I had access to a key, allowed me to sign for a key, even though I was not entitled to a key.

In my defence, I had previously been promised a key. And since I had already undergone a "key talk" in another prison, I genuinely thought the gate had been instructed to hand me a key.

The officer, also thinking I already possessed a key chain, did not issue me with one. As for me, being of the opinion that the whole issue surrounding key security was a bit exaggerated and that I would be able to take good care of it without the need to attach it to a chain, I did not ask for one. Instead I pocketed it and went my way. And so for the first time since I started working in the prison more than two years before, I was enjoying the freedom and the privilege that possessing a prison key brought with it – in particular the privilege to visit the toilet without "begging" someone to lead me there!

My new-found freedom did not last long, however! Midway through my consultation, I needed to respond to the call of nature. Now, being the "freed man" that I was, I made straight for the toilet without asking for help. It was after I had finished my "business" and stepped out of a main door onto the floor of the healthcare that the "alarm" went off.

The healthcare manager who was aware that I did not possess a key, wanted to come around to lock the door for me.

"No thanks, I have a key", I said innocently.

"I have just applied to security to put you on the list for the next key talk – so who issued you a key prior to that?"

"I was given one when I got to the gate this morning."

"By whom?"

"By one of the officers."

"And where is your key chain?"

"I am looking for one!"

"That's a security breach! I'll have to inform security. You have to hand over your key without delay!"

Action soon followed. Not long after I had got back into the consulting room, an officer arrived to collect my key. So ended abruptly the privilege of carrying a key in that particular prison!

I had to wait a few more weeks for the opportunity to take part in a "key talk" that restored my privilege of carrying a prison key.

12) MY ORDEAL WITH THE BUREAUCRATICALLY CORRECT CIVIL SERVANT

I n the foregoing chapters I have described some of the ordeals I went through at the gates of prisons and also within prisons where I did not have the privilege of carrying a key.

Prison officers as well as ancillary staff who are expected to work in the prison for a considerable period are usually issued with keys. Keys are not issued on a silver platter, however.

The first step towards being issued a key is for the applicant to undergo a security clearance.

Indeed, those unwilling to subject themselves to the security clearance procedure are advised not to seek employment with the Prison Service.

At the time I started working in prison in 2005, one had to undergo the clearance procedure laid down for each prison. Some prisons, in dire need of doctors, might allow one entry into the prison for a period of time, pending the outcome of the clearance. Others were stricter and denied one entry until one was cleared.

Initially, I did not find the need to go through the quite cumbersome procedure – the reason being that I accepted prison jobs only occasionally. Things changed around 2009 when a new system of prison clearance came into force in Her Majesty's Prison service. Dubbed the electronic clearance system, it involved completing an online questionnaire, printing the filled form out and submitting it together with specified paperwork to the security department of the prison where one was applying to work.

One was required to submit to the new clearance system, even if one had been cleared based on the old system only a few days before.

In the process of undergoing the electronic clearance, I came across an officer who literally kept to the very letter of the laid down rules involved in the clearing process.

After completing the forms online, I was required to present the forms with several other documents – my passport, my medical degree certificates, my medical indemnity certificate, my General Medical Council (GMC) Certificate, etc. – all in original.

I got all the paperwork ready and took one day off to travel the 80-mile journey from my home to the prison to submit the papers.

I thought I had done a thorough and diligent preparation. I had indeed taken all the required paperwork with me. There was a little hitch though – I had taken the originals of all the documents requested with the exception of my GMC registration certificate. Instead of the original, I had in that particular instance taken along only the photocopy!

I thought the officer would use his discretion and accept the copy for, after all, I could not be registered with the locum agency that had sent me to the prison to work over the last several months if I did not possess a valid GMC registration certificate. Even if he doubted my registration, he could find out my registration status on the GMC website. But he insisted on seeing the original certificate.

When I got home, I called to inquire whether I could send it through recorded mail. I would bear the cost of the return postage.

"I am sorry, that is not possible", he began. "It is required that all documents are submitted in person", he added.

I was reluctant to drive the distance of 80 miles to the prison just to show him the original copy of my GMC certificate! Fortunately, I was booked to work in another prison a little further away from that prison. My plan was to work in the new prison, sleep over and make a stop at the gate of the prison in question on my way home the next day, which happened to be a Saturday. I was aware he wouldn't be at work on a Saturday – some of his fellow security officers would be, though.

I would present it to the team leader and ask him to make a photocopy and write a note on it, attesting to the fact of seeing the original.

I made the stopover as planned. I explained the situation to the security officer at the gate. He asked me to give him some time to consult with his team leader on the matter. The team leader obliged to my request, collected the certificate, made a copy, endorsed the photocopy as requested and handed the original back to me.

I really thought that was the end of the matter. But no!

On Monday morning I received an e-mail from the security officer on the case. I could not believe my eyes on seeing the message it contained:

The security clearance guidelines stated that all documents should be submitted personally, in the original form, to him! Since his colleagues presented him with an endorsed version, I still needed to come over to show him the original!

Was it rage, was it exasperation that filled me on reading this?! The thought of having to purchase fuel to drive the distance to the prison, just to show the certificate, drove me almost mad.

I had no option, however! I had to put the process behind me if I were to get my clearance – without which I faced a dead-end situation as far as my prison work was concerned.

Without more ado, I wrote a reply to his e-mail requesting an appointment around midday the next day or the day thereafter. It was not for nought that I requested an appointment around midday.

My plan was to call prior to setting out on the 90-minute drive there to ensure he was at his post – to avoid the situation whereby I would drive all the distance there only to be told he had not turned up for work that day.

On my arrival, I waited about 15 minutes before one of his subordinates came to fetch me.

"Great that, at long last, things have worked out!" was his first comment after the exchange of greetings.

"All is well that ends well", was my restrained reply.

Next I removed the certificate from my bag and handed it to him.

After casting a glance at it, he walked towards a photocopy machine located in another corner of his room, made a photocopy and handed the original back to me.

Moments later I was back in my vehicle. I fired up the engine and set out on my homeward journey.

About two months later I received an e-mail from the security officer confirming the successful outcome of my application.

Though for a while, I did not return to work in that particular prison, the electronic clearance opened the way for me to work in several other prisons across the country.

For a while, I thought I had placed the issue of security clearance behind me – until my agency sought to send me to work in a Cat A prison. The Enhanced Clearance that permitted me to work in Cat B, C and D prisons, was not valid for the Cat A prison, I was told. For this I needed to undergo what is known as the Counter-Terrorism Clearance (CTC).

When the details of what it entailed became clear to me, I vowed, initially, not to allow myself to be subjected to that ordeal. Not that I had something to hide – I just did not wish to go through the painful process.

"Doc, you would do well to go through with it. The number of doctors who boast the distinction of the CTC test is limited. It will increase your chance of getting regular bookings."

Nevertheless for several weeks, I wouldn't budge. Eventually, however, I decided to go through with it.

In the Enhanced Clearance, I did not have to give details about my close relations. Not so in the case of the CTC. I had to provide details not only about myself, but also about my spouse.

The investigation did not end there. Information was required of one's parents. In my case, my parents are no longer alive. Still, I had to mention their dates of birth, where they used to live and what they were engaged in when they were alive. The questions just stopped short of asking me to give details of what both were doing in the after-world at the time I was completing the forms!

After going through the hassle of the CTC, I thought I was forever done with the matter of security clearance needed to work in Her Majesty's secure environments – but not until I was sent to work in the Immigration Retention Centre (IRC).

After working there for a while my agency informed me I would have to go through another form of security clearance if I wished to continue working there long term.

"Wait a moment! I've gone through the Enhanced Security clearance. As if that were not enough, I had to top it up with the CTC. I work regularly in Cat A prisons that house the most dangerous prisoners one can think of in the UK. Is that not enough?"

"Well", I was informed, "the clearances you have mentioned are for work in the Ministry of Justice. You will need a Home Office Clearance to work in the Detention Centres."

Apart from overcoming a load of paperwork, I needed also to attend a vetting interview. As I write, I am yet to decide whether to take this further step. So long as I have enough sessions from the prison, I have decided to take a "wait and see" approach.

In life one is cautioned never to say "never"; for a time may indeed come when I may decide to go through with it – if only for financial reasons.

13) THOSE INSTRUCTED NEVER TO ABANDON THEIR KEYS-- DAMAGED OR NOT DAMAGED!

Keys are not handed to prison staff on a silver platter. The first step towards obtaining a key is to undergo security clearance, the process that I outlined in the previous chapter.

The next step in the process is the "key talk".

The key talk is different for each prison. In some prisons it takes a few hours; in others as much as a whole day. The most extensive key talk/induction process I have experienced took place in a Cat A prison in the north of the country. In all it took five days, Monday to Friday, to complete the training.

One might suppose that, just as in the case of the security clearance procedure, there would be a national key talk procedure or system that could issue a key talk certificate that would be accepted at other prisons. At the time of writing, such a system is yet to be introduced.

The current practice is for every prison to organise its own key talk for its staff.

Among some of the things one is told during a key talk is never to expose or hand prison keys to inmates for fear they could take advantage of the opportunity to replicate them (at the prison workshop, for example). Furthermore, prison keys should at all times be hung on a specially designed key chain which in turn should always be hung on a belt which should be worn around the waist by all who are issued with them – male as well as female. One's attention is also drawn to the fact that the chain has the tendency to become snagged on the keys. One could usually disengage the tangle by dangling it and shaking the chain several times. Another fact that is also stressed at the key talk: in the unlikely scenario of a key getting broken whilst inserted in the lock, the holder should never leave the broken key alone but instead remain at the scene until such time that someone arrives from security to rectify the situation. One can only hope that in such a situation, one is in possession of a prison radio set – not everyone fulfils the criteria to be issued with one – or that someone arrives at the scene who could be asked to call someone from the security department.

I have so far undergone six different key talks – one in a Cat A, two in a Cat B, two in a Cat C and finally one in a prison for women. I might indeed have had several more key talks if my schedule had permitted it.

14) UNDERGOING AIRPORT-LIKE SECURITY CHECKS ON MY WAY TO WORK

At long last, I was privileged to use a prison key!
In this chapter I shall describe my daily routine in a high security prison where I am privileged to draw keys.

"Stop!" came the command. "According to the Offender Management Act, mobile phones and other communication devices are not permitted beyond this point without permission; any breach of this law may result in prosecution." The warning came from an automatic device just as I stepped into the forecourt of the security screening area. The automatic device repeated the message a few times before going silent, only to be re-triggered the moment someone else entered the hall from outside.

The first thing I do when I step into the hall is to take hold of three plastic trays: a large grey one for my clothes, a yellow tray about half the size of the grey one for my shoes, and finally a red one about half the size of the yellow tray for personal belongings such as belt, watches, keys, pens, etc.

I then go through a routine that I have developed for myself. First I remove my belt, then my watch, and finally my photo ID already provided by the prison, which I hang around my neck throughout my time in prison – a mandatory procedure.

Next I remove my thick coat – it is winter – followed by my jumper. Usually one does not have to remove a jumper but this particular one had a metal zip so had to be removed to prevent it from triggering the metal detector; then my belt, then my keys – both my car keys and home keys. Finally, I bent to unlace my shoes and place them in the yellow tray.

My tip to those who wish to visit a Cat A prison – you'd be well advised to check your socks are free of holes if you want to avoid embarrassment!

As I hand my items to the security official operating the X-ray machine in order to proceed to the next check point, one of the two officers asks the same routine question:

"Anything unauthorised?"

"Nothing unauthorised, madam."

Next I walk through a metal detecting arch similar to the kind one finds at the airport. An officer about five yards away keeps an alert eye on me in case the alarm is sounded. On this occasion no alarm sounds, so I am permitted to collect the trays containing my items, which have just been cleared by the X-ray machine.

If the alarm had sounded, I would have been subjected to the "rub down" search. Initially when I started working in the prison, I was always subjected to the rub down search, whether the alarm sounded or not. Now it is restricted to the instances when the metal detector triggers an alarm. One would be forgiven for thinking I was on my way to board a plane from Heathrow to New York, yet the procedure I've described is in fact my daily morning routine on my way to work in a high security Category A prison in the UK.

After putting my clothes back on, I take my place in front of a thick sliding glass door. Moments later, it slides open to allow me and others to enter. Yet even at this point we cannot move straight on. Instead we have to wait in an enclosure in front of another sliding door. Both doors are not permitted to remain open at the same time – indeed, it is against security protocol for the two doors to remain open simultaneously.

Next is a sliding metal gate that's biometrically controlled. In other words, it won't open to you unless it recognises you biometrically. One has to place one's finger on a device to be recognised. Once recognised, a light turns from red to green – only then is one permitted to go through the sliding gate.

On a few occasions the biometric device fails to recognise one straight away – particularly, I think, when one's fingers are cold. (Please note – this is not scientifically established, for this is just my personal theory! What helps, based on my experience, is to rub one's finger against the other fingers for a while to warm it up a bit!) Usually the device recognises the biometric features of my finger on the first attempt. Nevertheless it can happen that it takes more than one attempt to be recognised; it may work on the first, or the second or the third attempt. It may help occasionally to use a different finger, but ultimately the device recognises me and the door slides opens. Indeed, there has never been a time when it has failed to completely recognise me.

On one occasion as I was entering through one doorway, I saw a woman standing in the second doorway – trapped in it! Somehow the device had failed to move on after she had got into the doorway. She was stuck even before she could begin her day's work! Fortunately, I have so far been spared a similar fate. As I moved on, on this occasion, I overheard one of the officers who had been summoned to her rescue, reassuring her with the words: "Sorry about that, we've informed the technical team. They're on their way though it may take a while for them to arrive!"

Next, I have to withdraw a key from a key cabinet; as in the case of the sliding door device just referred to, the door to the key cabinet is also biometrically controlled. Keys in the cabinet can only be drawn one at a time. Thus when it opens to me on recognition of my biometric features, another person cannot draw a key after me whilst the door remains open. Instead I have to shut it and allow it to identify the biometric features of the next person before it can open again to permit another key to be selected.

I select a bunch of keys and immediately hook it onto a key chain which in turn is attached to my belt. Finally, I place the key in a specially designed key pouch on my belt. Keys must under all circumstances be chained to a belt.

Before the introduction of the biometric system a couple of years ago, we had to sign for keys at the gate.

Next, I wait in front of yet another door that is electromagnetically controlled. One has to turn a knob until there's a 'click' sound before turning the handle; one becomes used to the procedure after a while.

I pass through the gate into an open space and walk a distance of about 100 yards before being confronted by a metal wall with a huge metal gate. Again I have to identify myself by placing my photo ID in front of a camera installed at the gate.

Here too one has to turn a handle until one hears the familiar 'click' sound that signifies the handle can be turned to open the gate. I have to make sure the gate is properly locked before I move on. Failure to do so could trigger a security alert, which in turn could lead to a prison lockdown (more on lockdown later) and the counting of the whole prisoner population to ensure no one has escaped!

Prison security takes such incidents very seriously. In case I am identified as the culprit, it could lead to my being escorted out of the prison – never to be allowed to return to that particular prison again!

As I move from the gate and walk along an open space on my way to the main prison building, my attention is attracted by a spiderweb-like labyrinthine network of cords suspended loosely across the open sky of the space above my head. It attracted my attention on the very first day I arrived there for a week's security induction.

"What purpose does that serve?" I inquired from the security officer escorting me.

"It's to prevent helicopters from landing or hovering there, to photographically snap an inmate!" I was told.

Next to attract my attention on this morning was a dog walker on patrol with a huge German Shepherd dog along the perimeters of the prison walls, in the enclosure between a barbed wired fence and the huge concrete wall of the prison. The dog walkers are on duty throughout the day along the perimeters of the huge wall separating the prison premises from the free world. Anyone attempting to breach the prison wall – beware the fierce German Shepherd dogs on patrol there!

My attention is also drawn to the cameras placed at distances of about 100 yards from each other along the path I was walking. The cameras – they are everywhere! They are so ubiquitous in prisons that sometimes, when I enter the consulting room or visit the toilet, I begin to wonder if perhaps some are not planted there!

Finally I reach the gate of the main prison building complex. Among other things, the governor's office, the administration, and the healthcare department are located there. It is in this complex that various prison wings are located.

As a rule any main gate to any prison building boasts two different doors, each of which boasts different locking systems which require different sets of keys to unlock them.

There have been instances when I have worked in prisons where I draw keys, where my session has gone beyond 10pm. In that case, my keys won't help me get outside, because different keys are required. As part of the stringent security in place, after 10pm, a new or additional locking system comes into effect. Only a few staff members have access to that extra locking system. Thus, at night, everyone is at the mercy of those particular security personnel.

I have calculated that, in all, I am required to turn eight locks from the main building complex I have just referred to before I reach my consulting room. It is perhaps surprising that the door to my consulting room has no locks on it! A paradoxical situation, perhaps, in the light of what I have so far said about prison security. But it fits well into the security concept of a Cat A prison.

The lockless doors are thus there to allow the prison officers positioned just a few yards away from the consulting room to intervene swiftly in case a prisoner attempts to attack the doctor in the consulting room.

One should bear in mind the fact that when it comes to a Cat A prison one is not dealing with generally harmless prisoners like drug addicts committing petty crimes to fund their addiction. Instead it is home to generally dangerous and high risk prisoners, many of whom are serving long sentences, in some cases whole life sentences without the option of parole, for horrific crimes. For many such individuals who have nothing to lose, committing additional crimes, such as driving a knife through the neck of a doctor not prepared to prescribe medication the inmate is demanding, will be of little consequence.

Apart from the lockless doors just mentioned, in some Cat A prisons, prisoners who had already been searched prior to being moved from their wings to the healthcare waiting room are searched yet again, just prior to being allowed into the doctor's room.

Finally, I begin my consultation.

On this particular day I have a standard AM and PM GP clinic. This is the case on Tuesdays and Thursdays.

The situation is different on Mondays, Wednesdays and Fridays. On those occasions I do a standard GP clinic in the morning and continue on to the Health Care Centre (HCC), a hospital-like wing, to do the GP rounds before moving on to the Segregation Unit about 200 yards away to carry out a similar assignment.

Finally, around 4:45pm, my day in the highly secured environment draws to a close. I cannot walk straight back to the gate on my way home, however. I have to go through the process of unlocking of doors and gates as well as pressing on knobs to get doors opened, this time in reverse order. Before I leave the Segregation Wing, I have to open a gate myself. Then I come to an enclosure where my key is not able to open the door. Instead I have to press a knob for the door to be opened for me. I close it behind me and it is locked automatically. I advance about four yards and press another knob to get the door opened. It opens after a while. I close it behind me and it is locked automatically.

I then walk about 20 yards to another metal door where I have the privilege of unlocking it with my keys.

A further approximately 60 yards' walk brings me to another metal door that I can unlock with my own key.

A few yards later I'm confronted by another door that I'm unable to unlock myself. I press a knob by the gate and place my ID in front of a camera installed at the gate. Moments later I hear the familiar "click" sound, which tells me that the gate ahead of me can be opened – and I turn the metal handle that opens it. I close it behind me and it locks automatically. As I move on, my attention is once more drawn to the numerous cameras positioned at short distances all over the premises of the prison.

After advancing another 50 yards or so, I come to a gate I am permitted to open on my own. I must pay attention, though. The security protocol does not permit this gate to be opened simultaneously as another one

49

ahead of me, about 50 yards away. In case it is open, I have to wait until it is shut before opening my own. It is locked, so I can unlock my own.

I walk about 50 yards to the gate I just referred to. I have to look back to ascertain no one behind me has just opened the gate I had just walked through before pressing on the knob. When I press the knob there is a ringing sound, and finally I get the signal to turn the knob. I do so and move on, walking about 100 yards to the door that will lead me to the key cabinet I mentioned earlier – the cabinet I opened in the morning.

I press on a knob with my finger, and initially it doesn't identify me. At the second attempt I am recognised. I put my prison keys back into the key cabinet. Next to deal with is the sliding metal door. As I emerge from it an officer waiting in the hall between the sliding metal structure I have just referred to and the thick glass sliding door I am heading for asks in a friendly tone:

"Any keys, radios and cameras?"

"No, sir", I reply.

I then advance a few steps towards the large glass sliding door and I wait for it to open. It does so after a short while. I step into the enclosure between it and the one leading to the reception. After a while the one I walked through slides shut behind me. Moments later the one ahead of me slides open to let me through.

Next I have to show my ID as well as the key chain to officers posted in the reception area to ensure I am not taking any keys away. Checking for keys at this point might be considered superfluous, for there is an alarm system installed in the vicinity of the sliding gate that goes off the moment one carries a key beyond that point.

At this stage I am almost done with all security checks for the day! Indeed, *almost* done! One day, not long after I had begun to work in that prison, I was rejoicing that I had finally put the security hassle for the day behind me and could finally head for the car park and drive home, when an officer holding a clipboard with a sheet of paper attached to it, on cross-checking my name against a list of names on the sheet, said to me unexpectedly:

"Please head for security screening!"

"I beg your pardon?"

"Please go through security screening just as you did when you arrived for work!"

"But I am on my way home!"

"We perform random exit checks on staff; it is your turn today."

"So what is required of me?" I inquired, flabbergasted.

"You have to go through the exact security procedure you went through on your arrival!"

Well, I obliged without any further exchanges. I was not bothered *per se* about the check. My journey home was along a busy road, which got even busier during the evening rush hour. I had hoped to leave the prison before the roads became really congested. The extra time the check was going to take would prevent that from happening. Nevertheless I went through the exit check without any problems.

Later I learnt from a staff member that a doctor who used to work in the prison nearly got himself into trouble when a sheet of paper bearing the names of a few prisoners was discovered in his bag. He had noted the names on the sheet to serve as a reminder for him of outstanding entries he needed to make in their notes. It wasn't his intention to take it out of the prison; he had just forgotten to leave it behind. In the end he managed to convince security about his original intentions.

At long last my daily prison routine is over. I had, as it were, spent almost 12 hours "behind bars!"

Now I could head back home as a "free man" – not so the hundreds of inmates locked up there! For them the daily routine of their existence behind bars could go on for several more days, weeks, months and even years.

For some, the walls I am privileged to leave behind me at the end of my day's work is a virtual "end station" of their life's journey, indeed, of their existence on planet earth. There they have to linger, day in and day out, until death, the ultimate "end station" of our human existence, knocks on their doors to put the final full stop on their various life stories.

15) ALMOST LET DOWN BY MY MOBILE COMPANION!!

As I've already mentioned, it is indeed strictly prohibited to carry a mobile phone into any UK prison. It is not only prohibited, it is indeed a chargeable offence to be caught either with a mobile phone in the prison or attempting to smuggle one in.

Various reasons are given to explain the rationale behind the law.

Among other things, it is to prevent the camera and/or recording device built into them from being used to produce images or sound that could then be transmitted outside the prison and possibly compromise security or pose a threat to the safety of prisoners and staff.

Inmates, especially those sentenced for drug dealing, could use it to organise their drug-dealing business from their prison cells.

Inmates could also use mobile communication to organise their escape, intimidate witnesses, threaten their accusers, etc. ,

It is my custom to remind myself to check that I have left my phone in my vehicle parked outside the prison walls before walking to the prison gate.

One of the "never miss" questions put to a visitor who turns up at the prison gate is: "Any mobile phones or recording devices, please?"

Indeed, hardly does security fail to pose that question. On a few occasions, I had thought I had as usual left my phone in my vehicle only to realise on re-examination of my pockets and bag in response to the "never miss" security question that I had indeed forgotten to leave it in my vehicle since it was still either stuck in my pocket or in my bag!

Some prisons have lockers where one could, in such situations, lock it up.

In cases where the prison did not have such a facility, I was left with no option but to walk the distance (in some cases it could involve 300 yards or more) back to the visitor's car park to deposit it in my car.

Despite all the care I took to keep my mobile phone far away from the walls of the prisons where I worked, on a few occasions it still managed, as it were, to beat the stringent security check! Indeed, on a few occasions I had with all very good conscience responded with an emphatic NO to the routine question: "Any mobile phones and recording devices?", only to realise as I was going about my usual activities for the day that I had my mobile phone on me! The unzipping of my bag on arrival at the doctor's room to pull something out of it or the reaching into the pocket of my coat to remove something would have led to the chance discovery! Scared to the bone, my first reaction was to switch it off without delay – if that was not already the case. I didn't leave things at that. I would tread the path of further caution by removing the battery from the device!

On one occasion, I nearly got myself into serious trouble. Just as I was walking at the side of the nurse escorting me along the corridors of the prison to the doctor's office, all of a sudden, the sound of the ringing of a mobile phone could be heard coming from my bag! Alarmed, the nurse turned to me: "Be quick, doc, and switch it off! You're lucky no security is around!"

My hands shaking with fright, I hurriedly removed the battery from the case of the phone.

"My goodness! How could it happen? I checked and re-checked to make sure I had left it behind." I turned to her after taking the device apart.

"You must be careful next time, doc", she warned. "You could find yourself in serious trouble. Not everyone would assume you're carrying it without malicious intent!"

She did not have to point out the possible consequences to me! The experience of one of the cleaning staff I met at a different prison some time before this incident concerning her experience with her mobile phone was enough warning to me. Just as in my case, she thought she had left her phone behind in her vehicle only for it to be discovered in her bag during the gate search. Much as she tried to convince the officers it was an oversight on her part, no one would believe her. Instead the matter escalated! The mobile phone in question was not only seized, she herself was immediately escorted to the gate and barred from returning to the prison pending the outcome of further investigation into the matter. As she was told later, the mobile phone was subjected to intense scrutiny – including checking the contacts on the phone and also tracking the calls she had made or received with the device in the recent past. Several anxious days of uncertainty followed concerning the outcome of the case. Happily, in the end, she was cleared of any wrongdoing and allowed to return to her position.

It is no secret that despite the strict search regime, mobile phones still manage to find their way into prison, as demonstrated by a case that made headline news in September 2015. In the case in question, two inmates of a prison in Birmingham audaciously boasted in a "selfie rap" video they had filmed in prison with a mobile phone and uploaded onto the internet about drug dealing and violent assaults on rival gang members.

One may well wonder how the phones manage to get into prison. I shall use the case that follows to highlight one of the methods by which they are smuggled.

One day, whilst I was on duty at a prison, a nurse flounced into my room and began:

"Can you imagine, doc, what has just happened?"

"No, please tell me."

"Just as I was in the process of completing the standard healthcare questionnaire with the patient, all of a sudden the ringing of a mobile phone could be heard from down below him!"

"You can't mean it!"

"That's exactly what happened! Everything is documented. You can read my reception notes if your time permits."

"I know strange things happen in prison, but this is really beyond the extraordinary!"

"He had concealed it in his back passage. He forgot to switch it off!"

"Maybe he did switch it off, only for it to be switched on again by the pressure acting on it! So what has happened to him?"

"The officers in the adjacent room heard it, so they rushed into the room and took him away for further questioning! He will surely end up on the Segregation Wing!"

Later in my narration I'll describe a case of a lady who came to prison with a mobile phone, drugs and other items concealed in the anatomic passage unique to females.

Some also point accusing fingers at prison staff as a possible avenue for smuggling. One day I heard a rumour that the phones were selling for anything from £200 and above in the prisons. This however is an unsubstantiated rumour.

16) TOOTHBRUSHES TURNED WEAPONS

It is superfluous to mention here that prison authorities go to great lengths to prevent prisoners getting their hands on weapons. One way they seek to achieve this is by way of the rigorous security searches and checks at the gates the reader is familiar with.

Weapons may not only be smuggled into the prison, they may be manufactured in the prison itself, indeed by prison inmates themselves!

As part of their rehabilitation, inmates may receive training in workshops. Though they are subject to stringent checks when entering and leaving the workshops, somehow, some take advantage of their access to the tools and employ them in the manufacture of primitive weapons.

During a week's induction in a Cat A prison, we were shown a collection of crude weapons that had been sourced from inmates over a period of time. These included toothbrushes turned into knives, even razor-sharp knives, and a toilet brush sharpened to make a spear. Even if, in the end, such weapons may be described as crude, one can imagine the potential consequences of them getting into the hands of such a dangerous group of individuals as one comes across in prisons. Though I have not been eyewitness to any assault on prison officers involving weapons, they do happen.

From time to time, prisons, either in response to intelligence, or by way of protocol requirements, lock down the whole prison and conduct cell-to-cell searches for weapons and other prohibited items.

17) THE RISKY JOB OF PRISON OFFICERS

Prison officers' jobs, as might be expected, are not without hazards. It is not the remit of this book to narrate every incident of prison officer assault that has come to my attention over the past decade. I will only mention two striking instances in this narrative.

During my segregation rounds in a Cat A prison I had been sent to work in, I saw specially clothed individuals cleaning a section of the unit.

"Let's avoid that area. An incident happened there not long ago."

"What happened?" I asked.

"The inmate of one of the cells rang a bell to request the assistance of the officers. The moment they opened the door, he poured his excrement on them!"

"Disgusting!"

"Unfortunately, that is part of the dangers we are exposed to every day! Today it happened to my colleagues; tomorrow it could be my turn."

***

There was one prisoner who was kept on the segregation unit of one of the prisons I used to work in. My curiosity was roused because the prison officers seemed to take so much special caution when approaching this prisoner, and I wondered what he had done to land in prison. I Googled his name and the search engine immediately launched links to several pages relating to him. The gist of what was revealed is as follows: he was already serving a jail term for murder in a different prison when one day he attacked a prison officer with a primitive knife. In the process he inflicted a deep wound to the back of the neck of the officer. Not only was the cut deep, it stretched to the whole of the back of the neck of the victim. Thank goodness, it involved the back and not the front of the neck – otherwise the prisoner might have inflicted fatal injuries by severing some of the large blood vessels of the neck.

18) GETTING IN WITH NO GUARANTEE OF GETTING OUT

U sually, when I enter a prison to work on a given day, the thought at the back of my mind is that, unlike the prison inmates locked up there, I can at the end of the day's work get out and head home. That indeed is what has always been my experience.

I do not however lose sight of the fact that unforeseeable circumstances, however rare, could occur that might, even for a short period of time, prevent me from leaving the establishment.

This brings me to the concept of a prison lockdown. In its most common usage it refers to a course of action to control the movement of inmates. During a partial lockdown which may apply to a prison wing or to the whole prison, prisoners are confined to their cells for a period of time until the incident that necessitated the initiation of the measure is resolved.

Prisoners are routinely counted. If for whatever reasons – human error included – the number of prisoners counted does not tally with the official number for the particular day, a partial or full lockdown may be ordered.

A "full lockdown" may also be ordered to prevent a riot or unrest from spreading, or during an emergency. The situation may be serious enough to warrant the evacuation of non-correctional staff such as educators or supplementary staff.

A nurse narrated an instance when they were not permitted out of the prison until very late in the night. It happened when for a while one of the inmates could not be accounted for.

It got to a point when the prison called in special search troops to assist in locating the inmate. It was almost towards midnight that the culprit was discovered, hiding in the ceiling of a workshop where he had worked earlier in the day.

On one occasion, I nearly experienced a similar fate. A full lockdown was declared when one of the inmates was unaccounted for. It took well over three hours of searching to locate him.

Usually they are moved from their cell to the healthcare building. Somehow this individual took advantage of an opportune moment and climbed upstairs – don't ask me how he did it – and hid above the ceiling.

The full lockdown was lifted around 4pm, just about an hour prior to the end of my session.

19) TOP SPEED RESPONSE TO CODES "BLUE" AND "RED"!

On my very first day of work in a prison, I all of a sudden saw about a dozen prison officers running at top speed heading in one direction, I asked what was happening.

"It's an alarm situation", I was told.

An alarm situation could be due to various causes: fights between inmates, fire, medical emergency, etc. As far as healthcare is concerned, there are two types of alarms – Code Blue and Code Red alarms.

As the name suggests, Code Red has to do with the colour red. Indeed the Code Red alarm is sounded in response to cases involving bleeding – not bleeding from minor injuries and bruising, but the type that is regarded severe or life-threatening. It usually involves serious injuries – either self-inflicted or through a third person – such as stabbings, or deep cuts.

The Code Blue alarm alludes to the medical term *cyanosis*, which describes bluish discoloration of the skin due to poor circulation or inadequate oxygenation of the blood. In the prison Code Blue alarms are sounded or activated in response to medical conditions where the patient is turning "blue". It is usually activated in response to inmates who have become unconscious, have stopped breathing, are experiencing an epileptic fit, asthma attacks, or are discovered hanging, or found dead in bed.

On some occasions, officers will rush to the scene in their dozens only to realise that the situation has de-escalated.

On one occasion, I caused panic in the prison when I inadvertently sounded the alarm. I was shown the alarm buzzer in the doctor's room on the very first day I started working in the prison. "Don't hesitate to press the alarm when you feel in any way threatened!" I was told. What no one told me however was the fact that an alarm system has also been built into the healthcare praxis software.

On one occasion, I was writing my notes after the patient had left my room, when all of a sudden several officers rushed into my room.

"We have been told by the healthcare manager to check on you", I was told.

"What is the matter?"

"You have activated an alarm calling for help."

"No, I haven't!"

At that juncture one of the nursing staff rushed into the room.

"It appears you have clicked on the System One (Praxis software) button asking for help!"

"I was not aware that I could raise an alarm from the S1 software!"

"Yes indeed! An alarm has been installed into it. It can be activated by a click of the mouse. That's exactly what has happened – you have clicked on it, albeit unknowingly!"

"Sorry about that! No one told me about it!"

"Now you know, doc!"

With a sense of relief that I had not been in danger, they left me alone to continue with my duty.

20) THE COMMON HUMANITY OF BOTH INMATES AND THEIR SUPERVISERS EXPOSED

I have witnessed a few outbreaks of fire during my prison work. What is true in the community is also true in prison – fire may be started accidentally or deliberately.

Inmates may set their cells on fire as a form of protest, to draw attention to themselves or with self-harm intentions.

On one occasion, the incident was quite serious, to the extent we were all asked to make for the assembly point – an open, barb-wired yard, about the size of half a football pitch. For a while, everyone – prisoners, prison officers, nurses, doctor, other ancillary staff on the wing in question, shared the same common emergency as we awaited the arrival of the fire service. As it turned out, the fire was not started deliberately by an inmate, but through the overheating of a TV set in one of the cells; the inmates had failed to turn it off when leaving for work.

I am told that the protocol requires the fire service not only to be alerted in case of fire, but actually to be obliged to turn up, even if the prison staff manage to put out the fire prior to their arrival.

Once I was the duty doctor when the fire alarm went off. Moments later the sirens of the fire service could be heard. By the time they set up their system, the fire had already been extinguished. I was left with the task of examining the inmate who had been exposed to smoke poisoning. Happily everything turned out fine.

21) COMMON SENSE PUT ON HOLD FOR SECURITY REASONS

P rison rules are rigidly enforced – one may have to "literally do away with common sense" to enforce them.

A good example is in regard to prison doors and gates. They are meant to remain shut all the time. One has not only to shut them. In line with the inscription I referred to earlier – LOCK IT! PROVE IT!! – one has not only to turn the key to lock it, but also ensure that indeed the turning of the key has achieved the desired effect. I personally developed the habit of always shaking a door, after I had locked it, to ensure it was indeed locked.

The need to keep prison doors locked at all times has led to a behaviour among prison staff with access to keys that, strictly considered, could be described as bordering on the paranoia. For example, when a staff member gets to a prison gate or door and spots another staff member a few yards behind him/her heading in the same direction, even though it is obvious that individual would be passing through the same door or gate, the staff member who had just accessed the door/gate would with all certainty ask the staff approaching the door/gate what could be regarded as a standard question by prison staff: "Are you coming through?" The other would not regard the question superfluous, but would with all diligence reply, "Yes, I am coming through." Some do not even bother to put such a question but instead adhere strictly to the rule requiring prison staff to ensure doors and gates are not only kept shut, but also locked at all times, by locking the door/gate in the very nose of the approaching staff member!

***

A Class A patient once consulted me to discuss his sleep problems.

"Doc, I really don't know how you can help me. I usually do not have sleep problems, but the situation I am in has led to this. I am a Class A prisoner. The rules require that prison officers keep an hourly check on us. They usually open a flap of window on the prison door to peep through. Well, some officers do it quietly in order not to disturb our sleep, but others open and close it loudly, without concern for us. The moment I am awakened from sleep, I have great difficulty going back to sleep. I have hardly managed to close my eyes in sleep before the next officer comes to disturb my sleep. I was thinking that a sleeping tablet would help and cause me to sleep so deeply that nothing can disturb me!"

"Well, unfortunately, that's unlikely", was my answer.

22) JOY OF REUNION WITH FAMILY AND FRIENDS SHATTERED AT A PRISON GATE

One day, when I was on reception duty, the nurse on duty requested me to prescribe medication for one of the inmates she had just screened.

"If he is a new arrival, and not a transfer from a different prison, then I will need to see him first", I said.

"He is neither a new arrival nor a transfer from a different prison."

"What do you mean by that?"

"Well, it is a case of a gate arrest."

"What do you mean by that?"

"Well, he was released from the prison today and re-arrested at the gate!"

"That must be a joke!"

"Well, that's exactly what happened. As he headed for the prison gate, perhaps dreaming of his reunion with his family, he was re-arrested for an offence he had committed prior to coming to prison!"

"Why then did they allow him to go through the release process in the first place? They could have spared prison staff the time and energy invested in processing his release papers."

"Well, I'm not an expert in that area. What I know is this: during their time in prison, prisoners are encouraged to disclose any offences they might have committed that had not previously come to light. Whereas some choose to lay bare their hidden crimes, others refuse to disclose their past. When such offence(s) come to the attention of the prosecuting authorities, and they deem them serious enough to warrant arrest, they keep their intentions secret until the day of release. My understanding is that in some cases even the prison governor is left in the dark."

23) WE DEMAND *GOOD CONDUCT INCENTIVES* FOR ALL LAW-ABIDING CITIZENS!!

O nce when I arrived to work at a Cat A prison, I encountered a few other visitors waiting at the sliding glass door leading to the reception desk. I thought they had already been attended to so I pressed a knob to draw the attention of the person at reception.

"They are not letting anyone in at the moment", I was told by one of the ladies in the group. "There is an ongoing security operation." She added after a short pause: "I understand they are taking a category A prisoner to court; they won't let anyone in until the prison van has left the premises of the prison."

Not long after my arrival, about half a dozen well-armed police officers, some on police motorbikes, some in marked and unmarked police vehicles, arrived and took their positions at vantage points in and around the main gate of the prison. About five minutes after their arrival, and having closed the main adjoining street to traffic that led directly to the prison, the huge gate of the prison began to open slowly as though of its own accord. Next, three metal pillars built into a small road leading from the gate to the main street began all of a sudden to slowly descend into the surface of the earth, to open up the road. Moments later a large prison van emerged from inside the prison and drove slowly along the small road just referred to and headed for the main street. Just as the van joined the main road, some of the well-armed police officers boarded the police cars, others mounting the motorbikes. The police escort quickly assumed various positions – ahead, behind, besides – around the van. Soon, amidst flashing blue lights and loud sirens, the convoy was speeding along the streets of the major northern English city that was home to the prison, heading for court.

This security procedure, I was told, would be repeated on a daily basis as long as the trial lasted.

I reflected upon the scene for a while. The realisation as to how expensive crime or criminal conduct can be to the state came home to me more powerfully than before. In view of the huge financial cost of the criminal justice system to the state, is it perhaps time for society to think of introducing what I will term *good conduct incentives* for law-abiding citizens?

Indeed, instead of levying increasingly heavy taxes on the law-abiding citizens to finance those who break the law, it is about time the state also considered monetary incentives for those who keep the law!

24) PRISONERS CONSTANTLY ON THE MOVE

A considerable degree of movement of prisoners takes place on a daily basis within various prisons. Prisoner transfers take place for various reasons.

FOR PRISONERS' SAFETY

It could be for the safety of the prisoner involved. It could be that the individual involved had become a victim of bullying or harassment by gang members. Transfers could also be done as a way of separating prison gangs, one gang transferred to a different prison.

TO CREATE SPACE

Sometimes prisoners are transferred from one prison to another to prevent overcrowding or to create space in a prison already facing overcrowding.

DUE TO A CHANGE OF CATEGORISATION OF THE INMATE CONCERNED

Earlier on I mentioned the issue of categorisation of prisoners. A prisoner may be transferred from one prison to another due to a change of his or her categorisation. For example, a Cat B prisoner who has been re-categorised as a Cat C prisoner is transferred to a Cat C prison in line with the changed status.

TO TAKE PART IN A COURSE OR TRAINING

Prisoners might have a transfer so that they can do a course in another prison that might help them to reduce their risk of reoffending.

TO ATTEND COURT

During their time in jail, prisoners may have to attend court at a different location for diverse reasons – for instance, to answer for a crime committed within the jurisdiction of the court prior to their incarceration. Thus a prisoner detained in London may be transferred to a prison in Birmingham to be able to attend a court proceeding in Birmingham.

Once a prisoner who had been transferred from a different prison to the prison where I was working came for medication review. I wanted to ascertain whether the medication begun in the previous prison was still required.

"Yes of course", the prisoner said. "You don't even have to bother yourself – I am going back to my previous prison."

"Only after six weeks?"

"Yes, indeed."

"What then did you come here for?"

"To attend court."

"Indeed."

"I was in this prison on remand. During that time I was engaged in a fight with another inmate – I must admit, I gave him a sound beating! After I had been sentenced for my original crime, I was transferred to another prison. The court is now sitting on assault charges linked to the fight I have just referred to. I was transferred from the prison I was serving my sentence back to this prison to enable me to attend court. As far as I am concerned, it is a sheer waste of taxpayers' money. Do consider the matter, doc! I am already serving a 32-year sentence! They take the trouble and pain to drive me a distance of almost 200 miles to stay in this prison for a while in order to attend court, only for me to be sentenced to four months – to run concurrently with my present sentence!"

I could only hope that the authorities-that-be would listen to the advice of the convict; after all, as the saying goes, no one can claim monopoly of thought and wisdom, nor absolute right of virtue.

ACCUMULLATED VISITS

Prisoners serving their terms in prisons far removed from their homes may be temporally transferred to a prison near their family to give them the opportunity to visit them. After the accumulated visits have been exhausted they are transferred back to their original prison.

PRISONSERS NEARING THE END OF THEIR SENTENCES

Sometimes prisoners move so that they can serve the final weeks of their sentences in prisons nearer their homes. This is called "local discharge". Ideally, this gives individuals the opportunity to make links for resettlement, coordinate their release with their family and external offender managers before release.

Whatever the reason behind their transfer, on their arrival in a new prison, inmates have to go through the same reception screening procedure. The only exception in this case is that they do not usually need to see the doctor, unless there has been an occurrence of new medical conditions that may have developed during the course of their journey that need to be attended to. The prison healthcare electronic medical records are accessible to all prisons within England and Wales so the doctor usually re-prescribes their medication without the need for a personal contact.

25) PRISONER PROTESTS, CLEAN AND DIRTY!

While in prison, prisoners may embark on various kinds of protest. In this chapter I will touch on some of them.

Protest may be on an individual basis or in groups. Group protests can result in violent rioting, which can lead to human and/or material damage. Such protests could lead to wings of prisons being closed or, in serious cases, the whole prison being closed.

In all my over ten years of work in prisons, I have been spared a serious group protest, like the one that happened in HMP Stocken in June 2015, resulting in the closure of a whole wing.

Some prisoner protests can indeed take dramatic forms as the following entry in a prisoner's medical notes reveals:

"Hotel 5 (nurse on duty) contacted by Romeo 2 (Officer) as Inmate had climbed to the top bars on A wing with a noose around his neck. He was requesting to see nurse N but she is not at work today. Nurse D introduced herself and explained that she was part of the mental health team who worked with N and wanted to help.

Inmate looked down at nurse and said 'I want N'.

Nurse D explained that it was her day off.

Inmate then said, 'I'll have a long wait then won't I?'

Nurse D informed him that he could speak to her as she was also there to help.

Inmate then refused to respond and removed one foot off the bar that he was standing on as though he was going to step off.

The prison then went into command mode and nurse D left the scene!"

The situation at the gate of the prison where the action took place was quite unusual when I arrived there around 6pm to assume the evening reception duty. Congregated at the reception were about a dozen prison officers. I wondered, were they waiting for a bus to take them somewhere?

As usual I took my seat to await someone to escort me to healthcare (I did not draw keys in that particular prison). About ten minutes after my arrival, one of the officers ran up to the officer at the reception, who controlled the automatic gate.

"I want to get out here!" he shouted. "I've been here the whole day. I need about an hour to get home. How long are we going to be detained here!"

"Be patient my friend!" the officer at the gate shouted vociferously. "The security incident is still ongoing. So long as it is not over, no one is getting out of here!"

Almost 20 more minutes of waiting ensued. Eventually, one officer emerged with the "good news!"

"It's all over, you are free to go home!"

Moments later the officers streamed out of the sliding doors and headed outside.

Not long thereafter, a staff member emerged to escort me into the prison.

As I walked beside him, he gave me further details about the incident. The prisoner had embarked on a protest action due to feeling he had been unjustly denied the right to have a TV in his room. He had literally threatened to jump to his death. In the end he got a staff member to dissuade him from his actions.

Other forms of prisoner protests are as follows...

HUNGER STRIKE: Prison inmates may embark on hunger strikes for various reasons – for example to avoid looming deportation. I still have in mind an inmate who embarked on a lengthy hunger strike to avert extradition to his own country.

Some protesting inmates may refuse food but accept fluids. Usually such strikes involve both fluids and food.

Some just do so as a way of manipulating the system – such individuals may create the impression that they were on total food and fluid refusal; while creating the impression of being on a hunger strike, they would be secretly taking in fluids. Some abandon their actions after a few days while others carry it to considerable lengths.

As in the community setting, so also in the prison. So long as the individual has the capacity, no one – not even the most powerful man on earth – can force that individual to do anything against his/her will including the refusal of medication, food, drink or any lifesaving procedure. Thus, apart from monitoring vital signs – blood pressure, blood sugar, respiration, pulse, etc. – the hands of the healthcare staff are bound.

I have witnessed a few diabetic patients who had embarked on hunger strikes! In view of their underlying medical condition, it becomes a more delicate issue. Still, so long as they have the capacity to decide, there is little that can be done other than to monitor them and take any suitable opportunity to urge them to reconsider their decision.

Apart from regular monitoring by nurses and the GP, those on hunger strikes are regularly reviewed by psychiatrists to assess their capacity to decide.

On one occasion one inmate who had embarked on a hunger strike was transferred to hospital at an advanced stage of his protest to be force fed.

FURNITURE SMASHING: When I turned up to conduct the GP rounds on the Segregation Wing of a prison where I was booked to work for the first time, my attention was drawn to the loud noise emanating from one end of the wing – so loud it could be heard from a considerable distance. It was a newly built prison where each cell boasted a fine wooden bed, a writing desk as well as a wooden chair. When I first saw the room, it reminded me more of a student dormitory room rather than a prison cell.

"What is the matter?" I inquired.

"It's a prisoner protest going on. Initially, it was started by an inmate. In the course of time a few others joined in the action."

Bang, Bang, Bang! The loud noise emanating from the smashing and breaking of furniture continued unabated.

"What is being done to end the protest?" I inquired after a while.

"Well, for our own security, none of us is going inside. We have called for assistance of specially trained riot officers. We are awaiting their arrival. They will come in special protective gear to enable them to enter the rooms. Until that happens we have no choice but to put up with the situation."

"By the time they turn up every item in each cell might be damaged!" I exclaimed.

"Well, from the sound of things that's where we're heading for!"

DIRTY PROTEST: One day during my rounds on the Segregation Unit, my attention was drawn to the foul smell coming from one corner of the unit.

"We will avoid that area of the unit", the officer accompanying me remarked on seeing my facial expression.

"What is going on there?" I inquired.

"Inmates of the two adjourning cells are engaged in a dirty protest."

As we passed the area, I noted human excrement or faeces had been spread not only on the walls of their cells, but also on the walls of the immediate surroundings. Whilst there, a team of cleaners arrived to clean up the mess.

"Why not force the inmates to clean the dung themselves!?" was the unspoken question I asked. But I knew that was a non-starter. To do that might well lead some solicitors to bring a court action against the prison authorities, claiming compensation on behalf of the inmates for a breach of their human rights!

Some "dirty protesters" end their protest after a few days – some carry it on for several days.

26) SENTENCED ON THURSDAY, RELEASED ON FRIDAY!

Quite a good proportion of offenders are sent to prison to serve short sentences.

A record-breaking case was that of a lady who came to prison on a Thursday night only to be released the next day! She was originally sentenced to seven days. Prisoners usually serve half of their term; the remaining term is served in the community under licence. In line with that provision, the inmate involved was scheduled for release after serving 3.5 days. The implication was that she should have been released on the first Sunday following her arrival.

Prison rules have it that prisoners whose release days fall on either a Saturday or Sunday, are released on a Friday. Putting everything together, the sentence of the lady in question was cut to one day – in on a Thursday, out on a Friday!

At the time when she was being screened by the reception nurse, it was not clear how long she was to stay in prison. Since she had an alcohol-addiction problem, she was scheduled for a visit to the doctor's clinic to consider prescribing something to prevent her from developing alcohol-withdrawal symptoms.

When a nurse accompanied by an officer went to fetch her to see the doctor, they found her asleep.

Her first reaction on being told the reason for the disturbance of her sleep was:

"Please leave me alone to enjoy my sleep – I am going home tomorrow!"

"Really, has it been confirmed?"

"Surely, I have the paperwork here; do you want to see it?"

"Well, I do believe you. Okay then, good night."

"Thanks!" She covered her head with the bedsheet and returned to sleep.

27) COACHING COURSES FOR POST-PRISON LIFE

As part of their rehabilitation and also to keep them occupied, prisoners are offered the opportunity to engage in various kinds of activities. Some of the jobs they perform include gardening, packaging, working in the kitchen, etc.

They are paid a token amount for their activities, which helps them purchase items at the prison canteen. In this chapter, I will touch briefly on three of such activities.

ANIMAL SANCTUARY WITHIN PRISON WALLS!

In one female prison, I learnt of an activity that could be described as exotic.

"Please prescribe something to help with my allergy which is made worse by my work at the animal sanctuary."

"Animal, what?"

"You heard me right, doc; indeed I work at the animal sanctuary."

"You heard her right, doc", the healthcare assistant acting as chaperone added. "We do indeed have an animal sanctuary in this prison. You may pay a visit there one of these days when you have time."

"What type of work does that entail?"

"As the name implies, it provides a safe haven for various kinds of animals rejected in the community. We look after them until they are able to find a new owner in the community."

"What type of animals do you keep there?"

"Various kinds – at the moment we have two donkeys, 60 mice, some rabbits…"

"Mice?"

"Yes, initially the RSPCA [the Royal Society for the Prevention of Cruelty to Animals] brought 14 of them into our care. They seem to have been so satisfied with the care we provided, after they had picked them up, that they brought an additional 60!"

GET A HAIRCUT AT THE PRISON HAIR-DRESSING SALON IF YOU CAN!

As I was led around the compound of a female prison, the staff taking me on the rounds looked at me and inquired:

"Doc, do you need a haircut?"

"Well, I think I do, but my busy schedule prevents me from visiting the hairdresser!"

"Well, you could have your hair cut here!"

"Really?"

"Indeed yes! We have a hairdressing salon here. The aim is to offer apprenticeship training to inmates as part of the rehabilitation training to prevent them from re-offending. Staff as well as inmates can have their hair cut at quite reduced rates."

PRISONERS TREATING THE ELDERLY TO DELICIOUS MEALS

Once after my morning session in an open prison, I headed for a small canteen operated by inmates just outside the gates of the prison to get something to take away.

Just at that time a bus bearing the inscription of the Salvation Army arrived with about two dozen elderly citizens. On alighting from the bus they all headed for the restaurant.

It appears an arrangement was in place to allow the elderly and vulnerable to come there to have a warm meal for the day. The inmates there, staying in the open prison in preparation for their release into the community, were, as it were, contributing something positive to society.

28) THE PRISON DRUG PROBLEM

I llicit drugs such as heroin, cocaine, cannabis, ecstasy abound in prison. They get there through various means including concealment in the body. In this chapter I will cite a few examples of how illicit drugs are smuggled into prison and how they are traded amongst inmates.

SMUGGLING DRUGS INTO PRISON BY SWALLOWING:

An inmate in his mid-20s arrived in prison in the middle of November 2012. He was on a methadone-substitution programme in the community. His methadone prescription was continued after it had been confirmed by his community drugs team.

Not long after his arrival, at his own request, he was gradually detoxed of methadone. The detoxification was concluded in the first week of January. Shortly after he had come off methadone, be began to complain of abdominal cramps. That was not unusual for a patient who had just come off methadone. In such cases the doctor might prescribe buscopan (good at relieving abdominal cramps).

About a week after seeing the doctor, the patient attended the nurse clinic. Tearful, he complained of abdominal pain that became worse after eating – a condition that was preventing him from eating properly.

His abdominal symptoms worsened instead of improving. This led the doctor to perform various tests to get to the bottom of the matter.

At the beginning of February the patient consulted the doctor again. He did not only complain of abdominal discomfort, but also of being constipated, stating that he had not been able to have any bowel movement for ten days. He was prescribed laxatives.

About a week later he consulted a nurse, still complaining of being constipated. It was a nurse he trusted, as he later stated.

In the middle of February he confided to the nurse of having swallowed 80–90 tablets of buprenorphin (subutex) and 3 grams of cannabis at the time he was admitted to jail. He was sent to the A&E that very day. A CT scan performed the next day confirmed there was a package lodged in his stomach, happily not causing obstruction. He was discharged with a view to being seen four days later to attempt the removal of the package by means of endoscopy.

On the day in question, the patient refused to go to hospital. He was concerned that he would be charged with an additional offence. He was not worried that the packet might burst. According to him, he had done something similar on a few previous occasions and on all such occasions the package had passed without bursting. Several attempts were made to get him to change his mind – all in vain. Subsequently, he was made to sign a disclaimer.

Two days after he had refused his endoscopy appointment, he was seen again by the staff nurse, still complaining of abdominal pain. The nurse in question pleaded with him to consent to the planned procedure to have the package removed. Initially he stood on his grounds not to go to hospital. In the end however, through the persistence of the nurse concerned, he agreed to have the package removed. He was admitted to hospital on that very day.

Two days later, the package was successfully removed and handed over to the police. The patient remained in good health until his transfer to another prison about two months later.

"DOWN BELOW" CONCEALMENT

When I went to work in a female prison, I was asked to review a patient who had caused a stir in the prison the previous day.

Usually when prisoners arrive, they are interviewed first by the officers – then by a nurse. Those on drugs or those who need medical attention are seen by the doctor.

During the GP consultation, the doctor on duty noticed all was not well with this particular female prisoner. Her speech was slurred, her pupils narrow and fixed, and the doctor suspected opiate poisoning, injecting naloxone (medication used to block the effects of opioids, especially in overdose) to counteract the reaction. Still, there was no improvement and the emergency services were alerted. Within minutes she was whisked to hospital where eventually her private parts were searched.

According to her discharge letter, these were the items found: a mobile phone, spoon, needles, various powders (packed into a polythene bag) which tested positive for amphetamine, cocaine, benzodiazepine, heroin. She was immediately rushed to the intensive care unit for observation. Fortunately, she responded well to therapy leading to her discharge the next day, back to prison.

COCEALMENT WITH COMPLICATIONS

The matter does not always end without more serious consequences. One day, as I read through the medical records of a patient I was about to see, I noticed her abnormally high liver values. I wondered what had led to a sudden deterioration of the liver function of a patient only in her mid-20s.

"It's her fault", the nurse chaperoning me, who was already familiar with her case, retorted.

"What do you mean by that?"

"Well, she concealed drugs in her private parts when coming to prison. In the process the folio it was concealed in burst. She fell into a coma and was rushed to A&E. She suffered liver failure and spent several days on the intensive ward. Her liver recovered somehow but, as you have noticed, she is a long way from complete recovery."

AN INSTANCE OF PRISON DRUG TRADE:

An inmate confessed to me that he was engaged in the drug trade with the sole aim of building up enough capital for a business venture on his release.

"Hardly anyone in the community is keen to offer a prisoner like myself a job on being released. They may indeed initially be interested in offering one the job. They are eventually turned off however on reading through ones CV. It can leave one really disheartened."

"So how does the trade function?" I inquired.

"It usually goes like this: the buyer passes the message on to a relative in the community to pay for the supply either directly through cash or by means of a credit or debit card. After my contact in the community has confirmed receipt of the money, I pass the stuff on to the buyer."

"What happens if the buyer defaults on payment?"

"It cannot happen to me. As far as I am concerned, my policy is 'no cash, no exchange of goods'. Well, some do manage to convince dealers to supply on credit. They don't dare default on payment though – otherwise they may have to reckon with the retribution of the dealer."

EX-LEGAL HIGHS

I read the following report from the February 25, 2016 edition of *BBC News Online*, which reported:

"Prison inspectors are warning that prison is at risk of being "overwhelmed" by a flood of psychoactive substances known as 'legal highs'."

This brings me to the problem of "legal highs".

What then are legal highs?

They are substances that produce the same, or similar effects, to drugs such as cocaine and ecstasy, but until very recently were not controlled under or covered by current misuse of drugs laws.

They are also called "club drugs" or "new psychoactive substances" (NPS).

Examples of this group of substances are mephedrone and Black Mamba.

When I began my prison work over ten years ago, legal highs were not a problem. Now it has assumed endemic proportions.

Black Mamba for example is said to have become the drug of choice in several UK prisons. It has indeed become so common in UK prisons that inmates have coined the term "mambalances" to refer to the ambulances deployed to treat its victims.

Once I was called to attend to a female inmate who all of a sudden had lost touch with reality. Not only was she hallucinating, she was literally talking "no-sense". As it turned out, she had tried her hand at "Black Mamba". Fortunately we were able to stabilise her condition without the need to resort to a mambalance.

29) UNUSUAL AND EXTRAORDINARY PRISONERS

The law is no respecter of persons, even in pregnancy; no matter at what stage the pregnancy has reached, pregnant women may be sent to prison.

The same is true of disability. Inmates with various kinds of disabilities – the blind, the deaf and dumb, the wheelchair bound, the frail – have all turned up in my GP clinic.

Indeed, I would not like to find myself in the shoes of the judge or magistrate who has to decide on the cases of individuals with the challenging disabilities and impairments highlighted below.

PREGNANT AND IMPRISONED

Once a nurse came into my consulting room and announced: "We admitted a patient yesterday; she is not able to keep down anything. Please prescribe something for her."

"What could the matter be, food poisoning?

"No, she is pregnant."

"Really?"

"Yes, she is 30 weeks' pregnant."

"And they are sending her to jail!"

Well, doctors are not judges. Doctors have to consider the medical aspect. Judges, on the hand, deal with the law, and the law, as I said, is no respecter of persons. As a doctor, I would have preferred the justice system to allow her to deliver her baby first, before she was sent to jail.

But then I know that if one did allow her such an exemption, it would become a precedent for others – the blind, deaf and dumb, the wheelchair bound: all would be claiming exemption from the law, citing their various clinical conditions as valid reasons for postponing prison terms, if not actually demanding exemption from prison sentences.

I have indeed come across quite a good deal of female inmates at various stages of pregnancy – from a few weeks to shortly before the end of the term of their pregnancy. And thankfully, to date, I have been spared the situation where I might have been forced to play the role of midwife in an emergency situation! Not so the prison officers who were forced to assume that role to help an inmate deliver her baby in one of the prisons I have worked in.

One heavily pregnant lady, for reasons not clear to me, was transferred from another prison to the one where I was the prison doctor. She had, like any other inmate, to undergo the reception screening. It was during this process that she suddenly went into labour and the paramedics were alerted. The would-be arrival to planet earth did not want to wait that long and was soon pushing its head through the birth canal! The prison officers had no choice but to assist in the process. Happily, things went well. By the time the paramedics turned up, the new-born was already greeting the astonished medics who were left to attend to the proud mother. As precautions mother and child were taken to hospital for observation and returned to the prison the next day.

As I mentioned above, women are sent to prison irrespective of the stage of their pregnancy; the underlying medical conditions of the would-be mother does not usually serve as a hindrance.

As I write, I have in mind the case of a heavily pregnant inmate with the medical condition known as cystic fibrosis (CF), an inherited disease that affects the lungs, digestive system, sweat glands and, among others, results in the production of a thick, sticky mucus in the lungs with the resultant increase in the likelihood of chest infection and breathing problems. Even in the community where one is subjected to good air, it is a difficult condition to handle for ordinary sufferers. One can imagine the situation of an inmate sufferer who was not only heavily pregnant, but also confined for a good deal of the time in a small, usually, poorly ventilated prison cell.

At the time of our first meeting she was in the 28th week of pregnancy. As I found out later reading through her notes, she was remanded in prison at a time when she was about 14 weeks' pregnant. At the time of our meeting she was still on remand – the final court hearing being a few weeks ahead. (She was hoping to walk free from court which, however, did not happen.)

As the pregnancy developed so also did her breathing problems. At the time of our first meeting she had already been admitted to hospital on a few occasions. On each occasion she had been in hospital for several days, so she was in a pretty bad state at the time she appeared before me for consultation.

Two things immediately caught my attention – her protruding belly and her breathing difficulty. She was literally panting for breath. If I had my own way, I would have immediately declared her unfit for prison, opened the gates of the prison and sent her home to rest! The only thing I could do for her was to make sure she was admitted to hospital without delay. I put my thoughts into action and called the special unit of the hospital where she would be seen without delay and arranged for her to be sent there as soon as possible.

After about two and half weeks in hospital, she was discharged and sent back to the prison.

I met her again not long after her return. She came for a routine review of her medication. Though she still displayed some breathing problems, her condition did not merit an immediate return to hospital. In the end she was one of the few grateful patients I have come across in prison.

"Thank you very much, doc, for your help the other day. You know, they have been sending me to hospital so frequently, I seem to have become a nuisance to everyone here. But it's not my fault!"

"Tell me, why were you sent to prison in the first place?"

"I have been accused of a breach of a restraining order relating to my ex-partner, the father of my first child. I don't think I broke any order. I just happened to be in the vicinity. Even if I had gone even closer to his home, what does the judge think a frail woman like me can do to that strong and well-built gentleman?"

I did not want to place myself in the shoes of the judge in the case who might point out he/she was following the standard guidelines in sending her on remand instead of granting her bail pending the outcome of the main case. Considering the issues from the purely medical perspective and considering the charge against her, I would have thought granting her bail would have been more appropriate.

***

As in the community, pregnant inmates have access to midwives who visit on a regular basis to monitor them. They are transferred to hospital on the first signs of labour. In case of a planned Caesarean section, they are sent to hospital in good time to prepare for it.

YOUNG MOTHERS AND THEIR BABIES

I had a chat with a sociable, heavily pregnant inmate.

"What has caused you to be in prison?" I inquired.

"I engaged in a fight!"

"That's not what a heavily pregnant woman should be doing, is it?"

"Oh, the incident happened a while ago. I was just a month pregnant at that time! It was a fight that developed during a night out with my friends."

"And the judge couldn't wait for you to deliver your baby before sending you to jail?"

"Of course he didn't. I wouldn't be here otherwise!"

"That's hard indeed."

"Well, I was sentenced to six month to do three, for GBH.[2]"

"When are you expecting your baby?" (I had not yet had time to refer to medical for her notes.)

"Anytime from now."

"What will happen to the baby?"

"Well, my husband will meet me at the hospital. When everything is over, I'll hand the baby over to him and return to prison to serve the remainder of my term."

---

[2]   Grievous Bodily Harm

That leads me to the issue of what happens to babies born in prison. The case just mentioned can be considered as the most favourable outcome of an imperfect scenario.

Several things might happen to a baby born to a pregnant inmate. Just as in the above case, the baby could be taken away immediately after delivery and handed into the custody of partners, parents or other close relatives. Where this is not possible, the babies are taken into foster care.

Some female prisons, as in the case of the one where I worked over a considerable period of time, have Mother and Baby Wings specially equipped to cater for the needs of inmates nursing babies.

One day, the heating system of the Mother and Baby Wing I have just referred to broke down, leading to a temporary closure of the wing. The mothers were distributed to various wings of the prison. Not so their babies; they were sent to relatives in the community. Those who did not have relatives were sent to foster care. It took some time for the heating system to be repaired before the wing could be re-opened.

THE PARAPLEGIC

The dilemma of dealing with a paraplegic is highlighted in the entry notes of such a prisoner transferred from one prison to the one where I happened to be working:

"A paraplegic had been given a wheelchair access cell on D-wing, but in my opinion he would at least need a full disabled cell, as discussed with the Governor and Matron from the Healthcare Unit. It was agreed initially to locate him on HCC (the hospital wing of the prison) for a period of assessment, with a view to him being located, if suitable, in a disabled cell with appropriate support.

He is on pain killers long term, as has ongoing problems with shoulder and wrist pain through self-propelling his wheelchair.

Was awaiting appointment with wheelchair services regarding chair modifications, and further investigations into joint pains (in his previous prison) but was transferred! Will need re-referring at this point."

THE ONE-LEGGED PRISONER

Next I want to report on the case of a one-legged young man of about 20 years. Not only did he have only one leg, the fact that the amputation was carried out very high up the thigh, not far from the groin, made it impossible for him to wear a prosthetic limb. Thus the only way he could move around was by means of a pair of crutches.

When I first saw him, among the prison inmates, I wondered what on earth had brought him to prison. An opportunity to find out more about him came during a consultation.

"Why are you in prison, friend! Someone like yourself should do well to stay out of conflict with the law!"

"Unfortunately, I was caught shoplifting. I needed money for 'gear'", he declared, somewhat unrepentant.

"What led to the leg amputation?" I inquired.

"Gear, doc, gear", he began. "I became addicted to it when I was about 15 years old. Initially I was injecting into the arm veins. A time came however when the veins of the arms became damaged to the extent that I could no longer find any suitable one to inject into. In the end I settled on the large veins of the groin. Unfortunately, in the process I developed various complications in my left leg –infection, blood clot, circulation problems, etc. In the end the doctors saw no other option than to amputate it."

"One would have thought the harrowing experience I have just narrated would have persuaded me to put my addiction behind me", he continued after a short pause. "Unfortunately, that is not the case", he went on, "otherwise I wouldn't be consulting with you here in prison! I have indeed almost lost count of the number of times I have been sent to prison!"

THE DEAF AND DUMB PRISONER

One day, when I arrived at the healthcare unit of a prison I had been booked into, one of the first things I was told was that one of the patients on my list on that day was deaf and dumb!

"Deaf and dumb in prison?!"

"Yes indeed!"

"What brought him to prison?"

"Not very sure. I think GBH (grievous bodily harm)."

"How do you expect me to communicate with him?"

"No worries, we have made provisions for that."

"What do you mean by that?"

"Well, we have engaged the services of a sign language interpreter."

"Indeed?!"

"Yes."

"Is that individual travelling all the way to the prison for that purpose?"

"Exactly."

"I hope he doesn't need to see the doctor quite often – he will otherwise be a real burden to the taxpaycr."

Readers might recall that during the funeral of Nelson Mandela in December 2013, there was much fuss about the sign language interpreter who was doing a live sign language interpretation broadcast around the globe. Later he was accused by the experts of not being up to the task, i.e. not interpreting accurately. My meeting with the deaf and dumb prisoner took place not long after that incident. I could only wish that this interpreter was up to the task as well!

The latest blood results of the inmate in question revealed a situation the experts refer to as a pre-diabetic state. It is a condition in which the fasting blood sugar, that is the blood sugar level tested before the patient had breakfast, is found to be raised or elevated above what is considered normal, but is not high enough to be classified as diabetes mellitus.

The reason for the consultation was to explain the situation to him and to advise him on the necessary lifestyle adjustments he needed to avoid developing full-blown diabetes.

It was an exciting consultation, as I did my best to convey my message through the interpreter. Did he get the message? Well, judging from his facial expression and the gesticulations he made afterwards, I have no reason to doubt that was the case.

Just as he was about to leave the room, I asked the interpreter to demonstrate to me how to bid goodbye in sign language. She obliged. I then turned to my patient and did the same.

On seeing that he embraced me heartedly, shook my hands firmly and headed for the door!

That has so far been my first and last opportunity to consult in sign language.

BLIND INMATE

On not a few occasions, I have had to treat blind prisoners. Such prisoners are usually helped around the prison by fellow inmates who do so voluntarily.

Once, as I headed for the doctors' room to begin my reception duty, I bumped into the prison governor.

"Doc, they are trying to send a blind inmate to us. I am fighting tooth and nail to prevent it", he said.

"Why don't you want him here?"

"He is insisting on being allowed to come with his guide dog! I have told them we have no facility here to keep the dog. The last time I spoke to them about half an hour ago, there was a legal wrangling going on in regard to the legal status of the accompanying dog in prison. After all, the dog has not committed any crime! I am really hoping he doesn't turn up here."

I do not know the outcome, for he left the reception for another part of the prison.

THE EXTREMELY OVERWEIGHT INMATE

Prison cells are not made for the extremely obese. On one occasion I saw an inmate who complained of difficulty sleeping in the standard prison cell. What would one otherwise expect of a patient who weighed 32 stone (192kg); height 5.6 (173cm) with a BMI of 64.15?!

In the end he was referred to the inmates' ward with normal hospital beds. It was not a permanent solution, however, for that ward was meant for those with acute medical conditions. He could stay there temporally, so long as there was no need for his bed.

The immediate thought that came to mind when I saw this inmate was: "Why didn't this individual stay out of trouble in the first place?!"

FROM MALE TO FEMALE AND BACK!

In recent times there have been discussions on the issue of transgender inmates in UK prisons.

Again, I do not wish to engage in polemical discussion but will as before simply narrate some of the experiences I've had dealing with such individuals in prison.

One day, when I went on my rounds on the Segregation Wing of a female prison, my attention was drawn to an inmate with markedly masculine features. I had not yet had time to go through her medical records, so I was surprised to find her there, for the masculine features were noticeably prominent.

"What is he doing here?" I inquired from the nurse when we were out of hearing distance from her.

"Not a *he* but *she*!" was the reply.

"But she has the features of a male!"

"No, she is female", the nurse insisted.

"Indeed?"

"Yes, she has undergone a sex change, so 'he' is now female!"

"What is she doing on the Segregation Wing?"

"Well, no one wants her to mix with the female prisoners. So the only way out is to keep her on Segregation."

Later further details of her case came to light.

He was sentenced not long after he had undergone the sexual transformation – at the time when he had not officially been recognised as female. Initially "she" was sent to a male prison and kept on the Segregation Ward. After she had formally been recognised as female she was transferred from a male to a female prison.

After working in that prison, for a while, I was sent to another prison. When I returned to the work in the prison in question again, she was still being kept on the Segregation Wing.

"Is she going to be on the Segregation Wing for ever?" I enquired.

"She might have been sent to a normal wing, but now that is no longer practicable!"

"Why not?"

"Well, she no longer *feels* like a woman, so she has applied to become a male!"

"You can't be serious!"

"You can read his notes yourself! Yes, she has applied for a sex change again – she now wants to revert back to a male! The gender identity service of the NHS is now involved."

"Then she will have to be transferred back to a male prison!"

"Well, let's see what happens. First the process has to be completed."

After a spell of absence, I returned to the prison.

Indeed, the process had been completed. The patient was no longer Miss but Mr. Interestingly, he did not revert to his original male name, but chose to be known differently.

30) PROFESSIONALS BEHIND BARS

I have met prisoners of various professions and standings in prison – politicians, teachers, doctors, nurses, bank managers.

DOCTORS

There was the case of a surgical consultant from London, a native of a former British colony. Initially, I was not aware of his background, until during the consultation. Soon he was speaking as if he was the doctor and I was the patient. That prompted me to ask the question:

"Do you have a medical background?"

"Yes indeed!"

"A nurse perhaps?"

"A doctor, like yourself."

"Indeed!"

"Yes, I am a consultant; a surgical consultant."

"How did you land up here?"

"I am a victim of conspiracy and intrigue – not without a racial undertone! The hospital authorities wanted to get rid of me, so they concocted a plot against me. In the end I was accused of fraud – for billing the hospital for surgeries that I had not performed!"

"Outrageous, really outrageous! I am a consultant. I do not have to perform a procedure from beginning to the very end to claim it, right? You were also a junior doctor yourself. When you went to assist in surgical procedures, did your consultant or whoever was in charge of the procedure do everything?"

"I did perform the major part of the procedure and left my juniors to close up the wound. That is what is done every time, isn't? If the consultant or the experienced surgeon has to do everything, how can junior doctors get a chance to learn? Yet in the end the all-white jury believed the argument of the prosecution and ruled against me."

At that juncture, my thoughts went back to my junior doctor days. The orthopaedic consultant in the hospital I worked in had made a name in the area of hip replacement. Patients came from far and wide to be operated by him. He was not only good at his job, he was also a pleasant individual with a good sense of humour. Indeed it was a pleasure to work with him. After he had done the major part of the job, he left junior doctors like myself to close up the wound. In that respect, the consultant turned prisoner was right. How could I however be the judge in a case for which I did not have the full details?

"How long do you have left to serve?" I inquired just as the consultation was drawing a close.

"A few more months." He paused for a while. "I am preparing a compensation claim against the Ministry of Justice – for wrongful imprisonment, assassination of character and loss of income. Probably to dissuade me from doing that, they have relaxed my prison conditions. They have given me a special room. Now I am allowed to do practically whatever I wish to do – except of course leave this place."

"What about the GMC? Have they struck your name from the doctors' register?"

"No they haven't. Normally, that should be the case. No, the GMC just decided to suspend me. But they stopped short of striking my name from the register. That goes to show that the GMC also seem to be unconvinced in regard to the accusation levelled against me."

This interview took place in a prison that my agency sent me to work in only sporadically. That meeting turned out to be the first and the last with the good doctor. I have asked myself what happened to him. Did he pursue his compensation claim? And, if he did, what was the outcome?

* * *

Then there was the case of a female GP who was sentenced together with her dentist husband for their involvement in a money laundering scheme involving millions of pounds. The prosecution accused them of setting up a number of fake companies to launder criminal money and transfer it abroad.

She claimed she was innocent in the matter. According to her, her only role in the case was that she was co-owner of one of the companies her husband used for laundering the money. He was sentenced to nine years, and she for only three years.

Was it because she was not expecting a custodial sentence? Was it because of concern for their teenage daughter who had become homeless due to their house being repossessed? The fact is, she appeared inconsolable. Indeed, I had rarely met a prisoner who was so upset on her first day in prison.

* * *

Once a GP who was said to be highly regarded in the community was sent to the prison where I happened to be working on remand.

His offence? Here we go:

1. Under the influence of alcohol he threatened to kill his wife and their two daughters with a kitchen knife.

2. Scared to death, the threatened wife called the police. Moments later the sirens of the approaching police vehicles filled the air. Before their arrival, the drunken man ran into the street, armed with the kitchen knife.

3. Soon he came across a young woman about to get into her vehicle. With his knife pointing at the frightened lady, he demanded she hand him the car keys. Soon he was fleeing from the police in the "stolen" vehicle. The police gave chase.

4. As he fled he rammed the vehicle into several other parked cars on the street. In the end he was arrested.

5. At the time I met him, he was on a 24-hour watch due to the likelihood of suicide.

When I met him, at the time when his mind had been freed from the influence of alcohol, he could hardly believe that he had indeed committed the offences levelled against him!

BANK MANAGERS

As far as my memory goes, I have met two bank managers in prison – one female, the other male. It strikes me that both were quite young – either in their late 20s or early 30s. Both had a similar story to tell. They were lured into the temptation of laundering money.

Did the criminals take advantage of their relatively young age? Did they exploit the fact that at a relatively young age they perhaps needed money to purchase a home to start their respective families? This is however pure speculation on my part.

In any case, at the time I saw them, they admitted having deep regrets about their actions. They might have wished that the clock of time could be turned backwards, to the time when they assumed their respective positions as managers of their respective banks – but of course as in so many cases it was too late to alter the past and they had no option other than to spend their jail term in the company of seasoned criminals – murderers, drug addicts, armed robbers, etc.

NURSES

I have also treated a few nurses serving various prison terms.

The most high-profile case involved a nurse who is currently serving a life sentence for causing the deaths of two patients through injecting insulin into the intravenous saline solution administered either by himself or his unsuspecting colleagues. He was also found guilty of poisoning 20 other patients by the same means.

* * *

Then there was the case of a patient who came for treatment for lower backache. She began with a sophisticated description of her condition, which she attributed to lifting heavy patients over a period of 20 years.

"So you are a nurse?"

"Yes, indeed."

"Why are you here?!"

"Well, for doing some stupid things!"

After she had left, the healthcare assistant turned to me and said: "Do you want to know exactly why she is here?"

"Yes, I'm curious – in view of her profession."

"Wait a minute; I'll check from the HMP database." Saying that, she left the room and in a short while returned.

"What did you discover?" I inquired

"She was sentenced for stealing £4,000 from a vulnerable patient she was caring for!"

31) EXAMPLES OF HIGH-PROFILE CASES

FACE TO FACE WITH A MEMBER OF THE HOUSE OF LORDS!

Once when I was on reception duty in a London prison, I took advantage of my short break to read the latest BBC news online.

Making headline news on that day was the sentencing of a Conservative peer for expenses-related charges. He was found guilty of expenses fraud.

Not long after that, the first prisoner for the day was ushered in. I had not had time to leave the website before he entered.

"What is the BBC saying about the case?" he asked.

"Which case?"

"My case."

When I had a closer look at the man I realised I was seeing the same man as depicted in the online picture. I was indeed face to face with the very person whose story was making the headlines! He was a middle-aged man in his mid-50s. He was very polite, intelligent and well-mannered.

"They send us to represent them", he said. "They do not pay us properly. You claim payment for money needed and one is accused of fraud – the system is broken."

He was surprised he had been sent to a Cat B prison. According to him, he had been told he would be sent to a more relaxed prison.

THE WIKILEAKS CONNECTION

One day, as I turned up for work in a London prison, I was struck by the number of vehicles packed around the main entrance of the prison. The fact that some of the vehicles had satellite devices mounted on top of them and also the fact that some of those assembled had cameras on their shoulders led me to conclude that the press was involved. Indeed, it was an assembly of the press, both national and international.

Later I found out that the founder of Wikileaks had been remanded there the previous day. I missed a direct confrontation with him; for though he had been seen by the reception doctor, I was not on duty that particular day.

MADAM SERIAL KILLER

On my visit to a female prison in the north, I was asked to see a patient.

"She will be the last to be seen – for security reasons."

"Why?"

"Doesn't her name ring a bell?"

"No."

"Are you the only stranger in Jerusalem?"

"Well, I might be!"

"She is indeed a notorious prisoner, who caught the headlines for the wrong reasons. She and her husband committed heinous crimes in their home in a city in the south west region of England."

Later when I had the opportunity I Googled her name. The details of her case sent cold shivers down my spine – she was convicted of ten murders which she committed in collaboration with her husband in their home.

How true indeed is Shakespeare's saying, "There is no art to find the mind's construction from the face." How could I indeed associate the pleasant looking middle-aged woman I met in the consulting room with such heinous crimes?

32) ESCALATION OF THE BRITISH COMPENSATION CULTURE BEHIND BARS

Solicitors fighting for you!
"Experienced representation in Criminal Defence, Prison Law and Immigration matters, Prison Injury, Medical and Dental Negligence Experts – if you are injured in prison you can win thousands of pounds. Prison injuries could be caused in the gym, scalding in the kitchen, falling from a bunk, slipping on a wet floor, stabbed by inmates, tripping on a broken tile, injury in the workshop, injury on exercise, assaulted by staff or other inmates.

Call…

Or write to...."

Quoted from an advert in *INSIDE TIME* (the British national newspaper for prisoners and detainees), August 2014 edition.

Have you been injured in prison?

> "Speak to the prison injury Lawyers and claim the compensation you deserve!
> 100% confidential
> No Win, No Fee.
> Professional Lawyers.
> Specialist in Personal Injury.
> Call the Prison Injury Lawyers now on…"

Quoted from an advert in *Converse* (the largest distributed national newspaper for prisoners), Feb 2016 edition.

Are you due compensation for prison injury?

"Prisons can be dangerous places – but you don't need us to tell you that, you know already.

If you've suffered an injury as a result of being in prison, maybe in a workshop accident or an accident anywhere in the prison, and it wasn't your fault, you may be entitled to compensation.

We'd like to hear from you if, in the last three years, you have:

Had an accident in a workshop.
Had an accident whilst using the gymnasium.
Been assaulted by an inmate.
Suffered injury as a result of dental or medical negligence.
Fallen from a bunk bed.
Tripped or slipped in the showers, or even stairs or in the yard.
Call the free phone number…
If you don't win, you pay nothing.
People don't choose us by accident!
In the event of an Accident:

1) Report it immediately, say exactly where, when and how it happened, and note the Officer's details.

2) If there are witnesses, get their names and numbers and ask them to jot down what they saw.

3) Note the names of healthcare staff and what treatment was given.

4) Ask for photos to be taken of your injuries as evidence.

5) Contact – immediately on…"

Quoted from advert in the February 2016 edition of *Converse* (the largest distributed national newspaper for prisoners).

The British are particularly known for their compensation culture, which is based on the thinking that all misfortunes are probably someone else's fault and that suffering should be relieved, or at any rate marked, by the receipt of a sum of money.

This book is not meant to be a forum for a debate as to whether the assertion that UK citizens, compared to their peers living elsewhere on the globe, have a tendency to seek monetary compensation for misfortunes caused to them by others based on the premise "where there is blame, there's a claim" has indeed any merit and, if it has, whether that tendency has been spiralling out of control of late.

Whatever the case, one may assume that even for many a law-abiding resident of the British Isles, adverts like those reproduced above could serve as an enticement to seek compensation for misfortunes suffered as a result of someone else's making.

If this is the case for the general population, one can imagine the impact such enticing adverts might have on the prison population.

Apart from their criminal background, the fact that they do not usually have to pay for such litigation and also that they have abundant time at their disposal to invest in lawsuits makes them even more likely to act in line with the advert. That is exactly the case. Indeed, many a prison inmate is on the lookout for the least chance to sue the prison to claim compensation.

"Have you suffered injury as a result of dental or medical negligence?"

I have lost count of the number of instances when inmates have threatened me with legal action for perceived medical negligence. It's as though each one of them threatening to sue me has read through the type of advert quoted above. This is how they usually proceed:

"Can you please write down your name for me, sir?"

"What for?"

"I am reporting you to my solicitor for medical negligence – for failing in your duty of care to me!"

"You don't need to know my name to do that. You just cite the day and time of the consultation. Your solicitor can find out the doctor involved from the healthcare administration."

"No, I want your name, please!"

"No problem, you can have it." I would then oblige their request and write my name down for them.

Some go further and request my GMC number, threatening not only to report me to their solicitor, but to the GMC as well. I have so far refused to reveal my GMC number directly to an inmate.

With the above adverts in mind, does it come as a surprise that inmates are inclined to report the doctor to the solicitor?

Some solicitors on their part are keen to help aggrieved inmates fight for their rights. I still have in mind a case where the solicitor, probably after consulting the British Medical Formulary to ascertain the maximum possible dosage permitted for a particular medication, wrote back to the prison to demand that his client be prescribed that dose as well! Whether or not the client's condition warranted the prescription of the maximum dose of the medication appeared of secondary importance to the legal expert.

Below is an original solicitor's letter in an alleged medical negligence case:

> We *have recently received a telephone call from our client to advise that he has suffered injuries to his back as a result of an incident five weeks ago. Our client advises he has made numerous attempts to access medical care, and he has not received treatment in relation to his back problems.*
>
> *Our client advises that he has been suffering a considerable amount of pain for a period of weeks and we would be very grateful if you could confirm what steps you have taken in order to address his issues and if you are in fact aware of them.*
>
> *We look forward to hearing from you at your earliest.*
>
> *Yours faithfully*
> *Signed*
> *Prison law department.*

Though I am not familiar with the specific case in question, based on my experience as a prison doctor, I can with a clear conscience dismiss the letter as baseless. Even if the prisoner did not have access to a doctor, he would, with all certainty have been seen by a nurse who would have given him simple analgesics such as paracetamol and ibuprofen.

If the condition did not resolve and he happened to be in serious pain, he would certainly have been seen by a doctor on the same day or the next. If there was no doctor available in the prison he would have been sent to the A&E if his condition necessitated such a step.

The above letter can be regarded as the first step in the confrontation between inmates' solicitors and the prison authorities. It could be escalated further by the legal experts as the following correspondence demonstrates:

Dear Sir/Madam
Access to Health Records – Data Protection Act 1988
We are instructed by our above-named client in connection with a personal injury claim.

We understand that you hold records, scans and X-rays relating to our client.

Accordingly, we enclose an authorisation signed by our client and shall be grateful for either:-

1. Copies of all records, scans and X-Rays; or

2. The original records, scans and X-Rays which we will copy ourselves prior to returning the originals to you forthwith.

If you prefer to provide us with the copy records, then please would you ensure that the records are provided with a single record per single photocopied page, and that these are in chronological order.

This request is made under the Data Protection Act 1998. We confirm that we will be responsible for the appropriate fee (if any) under the Act.

We look forward to hearing from you.

Yours faithfully
Signed
Solicitors

Another common ground for complaint by inmates is in regard to the perceived reluctance on the part of the doctor or the prison healthcare personnel in general to offer them the same type of treatment meted out to the general population.

For example, an inmate may consult a GP to request magnetic resonance imaging (MRI) – a type of scan that uses strong magnetic fields and radio waves to produce detailed images of the inside of the body – for common back pain. If the doctor insists it is not indicated at that point in time, that could be grounds for the inmate consulting a solicitor – for allegedly denying him or her the same type of treatment given to their compatriots in the community.

For several reasons, scheduled outpatient hospital appointments may be delayed, rescheduled or cancelled. This could also serve as grounds for many an inmate consulting a solicitor for possible breach of rights to equal medical treatment vis-à-vis the general population.

It is not only the GP or prison primary healthcare that is constantly threatened with legal action by prisoners; the situation applies to the prison dentist or dental department for that matter as well, as the following entry in an inmate's medical record demonstrates:

"The dental treatment I got was inferior to say the least; I will leave it to my solicitors to sort out the fact that the dentist has broken the law."

The waiting list to see the prison dentist is usually quite long. The resulting delay in treatment could constitute a reason for an aggrieved inmate to solicit the help of a legal expert to pursue a case of medical negligence against the prison healthcare department.

"Had an accident whilst using the gymnasium?"

I have lost count of instances when inmates have sought treatment for various injuries sustained whilst using the gym. I have a way of distinguishing between those who just want treatment without any ulterior motives of seeking compensation and those who may want to make capital out of their situation.

I still remember the case of a prisoner who reported having a weight of 60kg falling on his chest whilst engaged in weight-lifting exercises in the gym. No one, apart from him, witnessed the event.

The inmate came to the consulting room literally bent over, hardly able to walk. He held firmly to his right side, acting as if he could hardly breathe. When asked to lie on the examination table to be examined, he replied:

"No way, doc! How do you expect me to do that under the present circumstances? I am in pain, in real excruciating pain!"

"In that case", I said, "I'll prescribe some pain relief and review you again tomorrow!"

"I thought you would send me for X-ray right away!"

"Try taking the painkillers first", I rejoined. "I'll see you again tomorrow. In case your condition deteriorates in the course of the day, we shall send you straight to the A&E with the ambulance!"

"Doc", he quickly responded, "be sure you document everything properly and carefully, for I intend getting my solicitor involved!"

"No worries, I will do my duty."

He struggled to reach the consulting room but somehow managed in apparent distress to walk out of the consulting room.

"Fallen from a bunk bed?"

During his days as a border in a secondary school the author of these lines had, at some stage, to sleep on the top bunk of a metal bed in his dormitory. Happily, there was not a single occasion when he experienced a fall. That, however, was not to be the case with a sizable number of prison inmates he had come across in the UK.

Indeed, over the period of time I have worked as a prison doctor, I have been consulted on several occasions by inmates who had fallen from the prison bed, usually from the upper bunk, though in a few instances some came for treatment claiming to have fallen from the lower bunk!

Even if the injuries involved are superficial lacerations, the victims would usually urge the doctor to document everything very carefully.

"Tripped or slipped in the showers, or on the stairs – or in the yard?"

I still recall the consultation I had with a 25-year-old male inmate in April 2016, just as I was in the middle of putting my prison experiences on paper.

He came to the consultation room struggling to support his weight on the right foot. He displayed marked swelling and bruising to the back of the affected foot.

"What happened?" I inquired after he had taken a seat.

"As I was having my shower yesterday, I slipped, lost my balance, and in the process hit my right foot against the wooden partition between the shower cubicle I was using and the adjacent one."

"Could you please explain the accident details more clearly? First you slipped, then you lost your balance – but how exactly did the back of your foot get hit by the dividing wooden panel?"

"Doc, you have to imagine it... I am falling, I try to balance myself; then bang, the back of my foot gets hit by the wooden panel!"

There was a short silence as I concentrated on my notes trying to summarise what I had been told.

"Please, doc, do document everything quite clearly. That definitely will not be the end of the matter. I am definitely going to have a conversation with my solicitor!"

"Well, it is up to you to do whatever you choose", I said. "I am more interested in the medical aspect."

"I think I have sustained a facture; please refer me for an X-ray."

"You need to be patient – I have to examine you first." Saying that, I made an attempt to examine his foot.

"No please, doc", he protested, "don't touch me; I am in agony – in excruciating pain. You saw how I walked into the consulting room. I really need either a pair of crutches or a wheelchair!"

"I think you have sustained a soft tissue injury", I said, "I don't think it is fractured. I have to rule that out so I will have to examine your foot."

"I am sure it is fractured!"

"Well the X-ray will provide the final evidence."

"Doc, I also hit my hand against the wall as I was falling!"

"Let me have a look."

"Here you are", he said, presenting his hand.

"Where is the injury you are referring to?"

"At the back of my left hand!"

"I can't see anything!"

"Well, it hurts – well, you can leave that out if it is not obvious to you!"

As I turned my attention back to the computer screen to work on my notes, he interrupted me once again:

"Doc, can you please give me a printout of your documentation!"

"What for?"

"I want to present it to my solicitor!"

"Friend, you have to be patient. In the first place the prison rules do not permit me to directly hand over medical records to you. You have two options – you can apply directly to the prison healthcare for a printout or else authorise your solicitor to do so on your behalf!"

Whatever the cause of that accident, one thing was evident to me – he was obviously delighted about the prospect of gaining compensation for the injury.

"Assaulted by an inmate?"

Prison can be a dangerous place for the inmates. Assault in prison is not uncommon – not surprising when one considers that it is a congregation of offenders of various categories and degrees in a limited space. Much as prison officers do their best to protect inmates, the inmates are subjected to intimidation, abuse, bullying and not infrequently assault.

Not all assault cases come to the attention of the doctor. Usually, prison officers are the first to get knowledge of such incidents – either by witnessing them directly or by being informed about them shortly after they have occurred.

Nurses learn of assault cases either directly or over the prison radio network. They usually deal with minor cases like bruises, scratches, minor cuts, etc., on their own and refer more serious cases to the prison doctor. In some cases, the nature of the injuries may necessitate them calling the ambulance straightaway. I still have in mind an assault case that was brought to my attention. It involved a hugely built inmate – a Goliath in every sense of the word.

During the day, inmates are let out into a large open space enclosed by a barbed wire fence. Called the exercise yard, it offers inmates the opportunity to walk around and breathe in some fresh air.

It was on one such occasion that the victim was suddenly pounced upon by a gang comprised of more than half a dozen strongly built young men. Much as our "Goliath" fought hard to defend himself, by the time the officers managed to get the situation under control, he had been given a really good beating by the gang. The victim was given first aid by the nursing staff alerted to the situation.

In view of the nature of the assault, he was sent to the hospital wing of the prison for further observation. I was later asked to examine him. Though as he told me, he managed to ward of the attack quite well, judging from the bruising, cuts and lacerations in his face, he was clearly given quite a good beating. I offered to prescribe pain relief for a week, subject to review.

"No, I can do without them!"

"You must be in real pain; take them at least for a few days!"

"No; I don't need them. I'm a hardened individual from Manchester, I have been conditioned to bear pain!"

Several months later I was interviewed by the police working on the case. The perpetrators were to appear in court and I had to give a statement. I was told that, depending on the judge on the case, I could be called as a witness during the court hearing. That did not happen.

I do not know the outcome of that case, since the inmate involved was transferred to another prison. I am very certain though that he would surely seek compensation for the assault.

Indeed, prisoners assaulted in prison do readily act in line with the spirit of the adverts cited earlier. Though I am not able to substantiate the allegations, word has it that prison inmates deliberately assault each other with the goal of claiming compensation! My experience with prisoners leads me to think it is not beyond the possible.

Below is another case example of prison assault quoted directly from the inmate's medical record:

Report from Officers on the wing that inmate had been assaulted by another prisoner. He stated that he had been stabbed with a biro to his head, hit with a hand and had also been kneed on the forehead, No LOC [loss of consciousness]. Alert and orientated. Pupils equal in size, reacting well and equally to light. No nausea or vomiting. No visual disturbance. Complains of feeling slightly dizzy. Cheerful and able to give a detailed history.

Bleeding present to forehead and right hand and arm. Swelling to left brow and small cut to the left side of his forehead. Scratches 5cm in length to the right side of his neck. Wounds cleaned and dry, dressing applied to cut to his brow. Advised to report any further concerns to staff at Primary Care Centre.

Four weeks after the incident the patient came to my consultation for a review. The cut to the forehead had healed, leaving an almost unrecognisable scar. He walked normally, without any visible sign of being unwell.

Though he looked well, he complained of experiencing severe headaches and feeling generally unwell and urged me to document everything properly since the police and his solicitor were involved in the case.

33) SELF-HARM, HANGING AND DEATH IN PRISON

SELF-HARM

While self-harm and suicide are not unique to the prison setting, they are also not uncommon.

Prison staff – be they prison officers, healthcare personnel or ancillary staff – are encouraged to look out for signs of self-harm and behaviour that may point to suicidal intentions on the part of inmates.

They are to report knowledge of inmates' intention to commit self-harm, either directly expressed or through suspicious behaviour, to the relevant quarter.

When there is sufficient evidence on their part to suspect danger of self-harm or possible suicide they are to take immediate action to redress the situation.

In response to such a scenario, a pathway is activated known by the acronym ACCT (Assessment, Care in Custody and Teamwork), a prisoner-centred flexible care-planning system aimed at reducing the risk of suicide and self-harm under the prison setting.

The ACCT process employs a multi-disciplinary team comprised of prison officers, mental health personnel, nurses, doctors, etc., to manage inmates deemed at risk of self-harm on a case-by-case basis. In the ACCT folder a record is kept of ongoing or significant events and observations, or conversations.

ACCT reviews are held by the multi-disciplinary team on a regular basis to assess the condition of the affected persons and evaluate the need to keep the individual on the suicide watch.

Methods of self-harm employed are not unique to the prison setting. These may include the following:

- Hanging, and self-strangulation, making use of bedding, shoelaces, towels, clothing, belts;
- Cutting, scratches, wound aggravation;
- Self-poisoning and overdosing on own medication, and on medication meant for others, as well as illegal drugs.
- Other methods of self-harm include wall punching; cigarette burns as well as swallowing objects such as razor blades, broken glass, plastic instruments, batteries, etc.

Talking of swallowing objects, the doctor is helped in his investigations by the metal detectors in the keeping of the officers. These are especially useful in the case of detecting objects such as batteries.

I recall a patient who engaged in self-harm through the swallowing of batteries, protesting the fact that he was not given cigarettes by the governor. He was sent to the A&E unit and an X-ray indeed confirmed there were two AAA batteries in the lower abdomen.

The A&E usually adopts a wait and see approach, with the hope that the foreign body or bodies ingested will be passed on their own. In some instances, they don't, necessitating surgery.

I have in mind a prisoner who displayed a long surgical scar on the abdominal wall. Asked why he needed surgery, he revealed that it was performed to remove foreign bodies he had swallowed whilst serving an earlier prison sentence in a different prison.

ATTEMPTED SUICIDE

I recall the tragic circumstances that led two inmates to become inseparable friends. The two shared the same cell. One night one of them was awakened by an agonising noise. Half asleep, he got out of his bed to investigate. As he later narrated, he could hardly believe his eyes at what confronted him! Hanging on a suspended bed sheet from a frame in the toilet corner was his cell mate! Though still alive, it became clear to him that he did not have long to live.

He immediately pressed the emergency buzzer. Not having the means to cut him down, he supported him on his shoulders and in so doing released some of the tension from his fellow inmate's neck.

Moments later, the officers and healthcare personnel rushed into the cell and began a frenetic attempt to resuscitate the man. Later the alerted paramedics arrived to assist in the effort. Fortunately the resuscitation ended on a happy note and in the end the two inmates became inseparable friends.

A CASE OF HANGING

A case of hanging still vivid in my memory involved a middle-aged inmate who was reported to have gone about his daily morning routine without any noticeable "alarm" signal in the air.

He interacted with his cell mates as usual and, after collecting his medication, he retired to his cell. In due course his roommate left to pick up something. He returned about 15 minutes later to find his cell-mate hanging!! He immediately raised the alarm.

I had just arrived at the healthcare wing of the prison – to work there for the very first time! I had hardly introduced myself to the staff when the alarm sounded. From all directions, healthcare personnel plus prison officers headed for another building. I followed them, hardly keeping pace with the younger and more agile staff members.

We left the healthcare building and raced along an open space into another building. On our arrival we met about a half a dozen nurses and prison officers resuscitating an inmate aged about 45. We joined in the frantic effort to save his life. From the ligature marks on his neck, it became clear to me what the cause was. He was not breathing, there was no pulse palpable, and his pupils were fixed.

Not long after our arrival, the paramedics also arrived. That particular prison happens to almost border the main hospital so the ambulance took only a few minutes to arrive. This was followed by about half an hour of frenetic attempts at resuscitation.

Still not responding to our efforts, the man was taken into the care of the paramedics who continued the resuscitation effort as they went. About half an hour after they had left, word reached me that the man had been pronounced dead.

Though that was my very first contact with the dead, by reason of me being the last doctor to see him, I was interviewed on the matter on that same day.

As in the case of all tragic deaths in prison, an inquest was held. Initially I was invited to attend the inquest but, after informing them of the circumstances under which I saw him, I was told I did not need to attend.

DEATH IN CUSTODY

Death in custody, whether expected (natural causes) or unexpected (tragic circumstances), are independently investigated by the Prison and Probation Ombudsman (PPO).

Death in prison, even if through natural causes, brings with it a lot of paperwork. Sadly, unnatural deaths, especially through suicide, are not uncommon in prison. Most forms of suicide are by way of hanging.

As I mentioned earlier, those who openly express suicide inclinations, or who by way of their behaviour are deemed at risk of suicide, are placed on the ACCT.

This can result in the person suspected of suicidal intentions being placed on a suicide watch. Depending on the individual case, the watch can be around the clock or involve regular checks at various times – 15minutes, 30 minutes, hourly intervals – as the case may be.

Sadly, it is not always easy to prevent those who are determined to end their lives from doing so.

I have been witness to not a few instances when inmates who had been on constant watch carried out their threats to end their own lives just at the time when the time interval of the watch had been prolonged or when the inmates had been completely removed from the watch status.

INQUEST

Every death in prison or police custody is subject to an inquest. On one occasion I had to appear before such a judicial inquiry into a death in custody.

The sad event occurred in a prison where I work only sporadically.

On one of the few days in the year that I worked there, my duty was to carry out what was termed a five-day review of patients on an alcohol and/or methadone detoxification regime.

The aim of the clinic is for the doctor to ascertain how inmates addicted to various drugs are coping with the corresponding detoxification regime prescribed for them on their arrival five days earlier.

Just as the patient was about to leave my clinic after the assessment, he turned to the nurse chaperoning me and reported that he was feeling depressed despite being on an antidepressant and requested an increase in dosage of the drug in question.

At that stage the nurse turned to me and inquired whether I would be prepared to do so. She added that she was familiar with the patient and was aware he had a mental health review in a few days' time. I realised that he was on the least possible dose of the medication in question so I agreed to increase the dosage pending the planned mental health review. That would turn out to be my first and last meeting with the individual concerned.

As I later found from his notes, his mental state deteriorated further. Concerned that he could possibly take his life, he was placed on an ACCT. Just as everyone thought he had turned the corner as far as his depressive state of mind was concerned, he was discovered one morning hanging in his cell. The sad event occurred about four weeks after I had seen him.

As it turned out I was the last doctor to see him prior to his death. Because of that, I was invited to the coroner's court. Initially, I was reluctant to attend and requested to be allowed to provide just a written statement.

In the first place, I was concerned about the loss of income that it would entail. (Though I was to be compensated, the amount involved did not match what I would otherwise earn working as a doctor.)

Secondly, my meeting with him on that day had centred mainly on the fact that he was coping with his alcohol detoxification and not on issues relating to his mental state. In the end I had to attend on the insistence of the court.

I do not know how much my presence helped the coroner in his investigations, for apart from stating what the reader is already aware of, there was nothing else I could contribute to the process.

That has been my first and, thus far, my last appearance at an inquest.

34) IMMIGRATION RETENTION CENTRE BULLETIN

Apart from working in typical prisons, I have also worked in Immigration Removal Centres. When I began working in such establishments about a decade ago, they were known as Immigration Detention Centres.

After a long absence, I returned to work there only to notice the change of name. I was told the authorities were not comfortable with the terminology, the word *Detention* especially, so they opted for *Removal*. As far as I am concerned, it is only a matter of semantics, for hardly anything has changed in the manner the inmates are treated.

For those not conversant with IRCs, they serve as holding centres for foreign nationals who are either awaiting a decision on their asylum applications or who are awaiting deportation following a failed application.

Apart from the named group of individuals, foreign nationals who might have overstayed their visas or who managed through whatever means to find their way into the country illegally, when caught in the community, are detained at the IRC pending their deportation or the outcome of their legal challenge to the decision to deport them.

Though it is not formally regarded as a prison, the IRC does indeed bear the hallmark of a prison. As far as freedom of movement is concerned, even inmates of the open prison are better placed. For whereas Class D prisoners are permitted under some conditions, to go out into the community to work, inmates of the IRC are not permitted to do so.

What struck me the first time I was sent to work in an IRC, then known as IDC, was that among the inmates were children of school-going age and in some instances even infants.

Indeed, at the time I worked there, a few of them told me they were in the process of preparing for the GCSE, having been sent there with their parents! A kind of school had been set up there to educate the children and enable those inmates I referred to, to continue their preparation towards their examination. Needless to say, it was not the appropriate environment for children to be educated.

When I returned to work there several years later, the absence of children was noticeable.

"Are you no longer keeping children here?" I inquired.

"Indeed. In December 2010 the government of the day announced the closure of the family wing; we have indeed had no children in this facility since 2011."

The impression I gained working there was that the majority of the inmates were fighting tooth and nail to avert deportation, with each of them bringing up excuses, or concocting stories, or looking for proof to justify their ongoing stay in the country.

In the following sections, I will narrate the cases of a few of the inmates I came across.

MAIN BREADWINNER OF EXTENDED AFRICAN FAMILY THREATENED WITH DEPORTATION

A lady from Ghana who had been arrested just a day prior to my meeting her was inconsolable! She was at work when she was arrested.

"I was doing a well-paid job, doc! I do not know whether my arrest was a result of a tip off to the police from someone who was jealous of me. In any case, I was at work when the immigration authorities arrived to demand my papers! This is a brutal world, doc. I am the main breadwinner of my extended family in Ghana. What will happen to me and my family should I be deported!"

THE ALLEGED PROSTITUTION RING LEADER WHO SUDDENLY TURNED DEAF AND DUMB

Then there was the case of the Chinese lady of about 35 who pretended to be deaf and mute on her arrival at the IRC – at least everyone, with the exception of herself, was convinced that was the case.

She had been arrested on issues related not only to her immigration status, but also her alleged role as the leader of a prostitution ring.

According to the police report, several witnesses testified to the fact that she had no impairment of hearing or of speech, that she had been managing her business without any problems, and that she had all of a sudden become deaf and dumb on her arrival at the IRC. They sent her to the GP for review. I did not know the expectation they had from the GP!

FACING DEPORTATION AFTER 30 YEARS' RESIDENCY

I treated an Indian national in his 60s who was arrested for overstaying his visa.

"Doc, I arrived in this country over 30 years ago! I have not been idle during those years. With a small capital, I set up a business that has expanded greatly, with an annual turnover of millions of pounds!"

"Why didn't you regularise your stay during that period?"

"I applied to the Home Office. I failed to pursue my application but then, in my defence, I heard nothing from them. Those were the days when no one bothered over such things. I managed to register my company. I was paying my taxes and I thought that was it – until I started receiving letters from the Home Office concerning my immigration status. Then, one day, the Home Office people knocked on my door and brought me here."

"I am going nowhere!" he resumed after a short pause. "I have hired top immigration solicitors to pursue my case. They want to deport me and get hold of my property. I can't let that happen!"

I must stress that I am just reporting what he told me. Whether it was the truth or a fabrication, I am not in a position to judge. The impression he made on me however was that he appeared to be sincere and his story credible.

I could only wish him well and hope the matter was settled in the shortest possible time. Not only did he have a heart condition, he was also a diabetic, requiring insulin. His stressful situation did not augur well for his health.

A DRAMATIC CHANGE OF HEART

Then there was the case of a pregnant lady from Africa who obtained a genuine visa from the UK consulate while still in her native country. In due time however it came to the attention of the high commission that the paperwork she presented to support her application had been forged. She was arrested on her arrival at Heathrow and threatened with deportation.

Initially, she consented to deportation. Probably due to lack of space on the next available flight to her home country, she was not immediately sent back home; instead, she was sent to the IRC. In due course she had access to a solicitor. From then on the case took a different turn.

"I never consented to return to my country", she stated emphatically. "The words were placed in my mouth – under duress", she claimed. "I face a real threat to my life in my country. I betrayed a drug-smuggling ring to the authorities in my hometown. In retribution, the gang kidnapped and gang-raped me, and this caused my pregnancy. They did not leave matters at that, however; they kept sending me death threats. Indeed, on one occasion they attacked me on the street. I was only rescued by bystanders!"

When I returned to work there a few weeks later, I noticed that she had indeed been released into the community – pending the outcome of her application.

A LONG OVERDUE DOCTOR'S APPOINMENT TO THE RESCUE!

Then there was the case of a lady who had eye surgery in the community about 18 months prior to her detention. According to the medical report obtained from her GP by the IRC, she was due for a follow-up health check a few weeks after the procedure. She failed however to turn up.

Faced with the threat of deportation, all of a sudden the eye treatment became an issue in her defence. She wanted to be released on medical grounds – so she could get her sutures removed!

A YEARNING TO RETURN HOME SADDLED WITH BUREAUCRATIC HURDLES

As the above examples demonstrate, the majority of those I met were fighting hard to avert deportation.

There were a few of what I will term role-reversal cases. Indeed, I came across inmates who, despite having a burning desire to be permitted to leave the country at the next opportunity, could not do so for various reasons.

The main stumbling block usually revolved around obtaining the requisite travel documents to facilitate their deportation.

Having lived in the country for considerable periods of time, their travel documents had expired or in some cases gone missing or both. Getting replacement documents from their country representatives in the UK could be a wearisome matter, which could take weeks if not months to resolve.

Curiously, I gained the impression that some of the inmates regarded healthcare workers like myself with suspicion, considering us not as people who are there to help them but rather as collaborators with the immigration authorities.

35) A BABYLON OF LANGUAGES

Inmates of the IRC can be aptly regarded as a microcosm of the world population. This was especially apparent during one particular duty at the IRC – when the background of the inmates I saw gave me special food for thought. Usually, the majority of inmates who come for consultation on a particular day, though from various countries on the planet, are at home in the English language. On the particular day, however, things were quite different. One after the other, each of the eight or so patients in my clinic signalled to me on entering the consulting room that they could not communicate in English. At times like this we make use of a telephone translator service, which involves a special telephone that enables two people to use it at the same time.

First I had to dial a number, then give a language code, and eventually I was connected to a translator. The first patient for the day was a Chinese lady who spoke in Mandarin. It was around 9:30am on a Sunday.

The call handler seemed to struggle to find an appropriate translator for we had to wait unusually long to be connected to a translator. Eventually the voice of a lady came through.

My first impression was that I was speaking with someone who had just awakened from sleep. I could hardly make sense of the murmuring sounds that came from her. It was indeed quite a struggle getting her to understand what I wanted her to translate. In the end we managed to put the ordeal behind us.

After the translator had put down the phone, both of us burst into laughter.

"Sleep, slee – lee – ping?" My patient made use of the little English she commanded to express her thoughts about the translator.

The next patient was not very different from the other as far as her knowledge of English was concerned. Hardly had she taken her place on the chair near to my desk than she said: "No English!"

What language?"

"Kurdish."

"Okay, I will request a Kurdish translator."

"Kurmanji ; Kurmanji Kurd please!"

"What? I thought every Kurd speaks Kurdish?"

"Different, different Kurdish: I Kurmanji – Kurdish."

"Kurmanji?"

"Yes Kurmanji. Not Sorani, Kurdish; not Pehlewani Kurdish!"

"But – you – understand all three?"

"Yes… yes, but... better Kurmanji… sir!"

Well eventually I got a Kurmanji-Kurd translator for her.

On my part, I was grateful to her for helping to fine-tune my knowledge in matters concerning the Kurdish language.

The next person to appear before me was a lady from Eritrea. In her case I thought she spoke the Eritrean language. "No, Tigrinya, please. There is no Eritrean language", she pointed out to me.

Next in line was a lady from India who also requested a translator. I thought she spoke Hindi, the main language of India.

"No please, no Hindi translator Punjabi, please."

A lady from the Ukraine was the next to request a translator.

Although it rarely happens, on this occasion, just as we were in the middle of consultation, the telephone connection was lost. I re-dialled the number hoping to be re-connected to the translator, but no, the call handler informed me he too had lost the connection with her. He would therefore look for the next available translator. After asking me to hold on for a while, his voice could be heard again: "Unfortunately you may have to hang on for a while; I am having difficulty finding a Ukraine translator."

"Russia okay; Russia okay", interjected the patient who had been following the conversation.

"But you are from Ukraine?"

"Yes; but every Ukrainian speak Russia." She added: "People from Ukraine; people from Russia, like brothers and sisters!"

It was at the time when the Ukraine and Russia were at loggerheads in regard to the status of eastern Ukraine – a conflict that up till then had led to considerable loss of life.

If, as this lady was saying, the two countries were like "brothers and sisters" then why all the bloodshed, I pondered!

Well, I realised that my reasoning was too simplistic. Aren't conflicts going on all the time between close relatives, even between brothers and sisters?

After the extraordinary session involving what I have termed a *Babylon of languages* was over, I sat down to ponder over the matter of the different languages of our world. Some I had just heard were high pitched, others low pitched, while still others were in between the two extremes. Some were spoken with some degree of force, with strident assertiveness; some softly. Some sounded as if they were whistling; some as if they were drumming. To those who understood them, it was a means of communication, a means of conveying important messages and information.

To someone like myself who is unfamiliar with the languages involved, the speakers made practically no sense. Those speaking these languages might have been insulting me, even making derogatory remarks about me; yet there I sat, unaware of what was going on around me.

Languages – what a mystery in the even greater mystery of our human existence!

PART TWO
HEALTH MATTERS

36) WELCOME TO PRISON HEALTHCARE

The health care unit of a prison is organised along the lines of the community GP practice or surgery. Depending on the prison population, a prison may have one, two or even more GP clinics running simultaneously on a particular day. Prisons usually have at least one resident GP – the remaining doctors, like the author of these lines, being locum doctors booked to work there on an on-demand basis.

My personal observation, after working as a prison doctor for more than ten years, is that increasingly prisons are experiencing difficulties recruiting their own doctors, making them resort to locum GPs like me. The result is that there is a frequent coming and going of new doctors, a fact that does not augur well for continuity of care.

Nurses play a very important role in the running of the prison healthcare department. Indeed, many prison healthcare departments are nurse-led. They not only perform duties discharged by their counterparts in a community surgery such as taking blood, administering injections, dressing wounds, etc., but are also pivotal in case of healthcare emergencies such as heart attacks, instances of hanging, asthma attacks, etc.

As I have mentioned, many prisons rely on doctors employed on a temporary basis to run their clinics. In view of their temporary status, locum doctors like me are not issued with prison radio handsets over which alarms and healthcare emergencies are announced. The situation is different with the nursing staff; many of the leading nurses are on permanent or long-term contracts, so have access to the prison radio.

In case of medical emergencies within the prison, such as suspected heart attacks, inmates found hanging, inmates discovered unconscious, etc., nurses equipped with prison radio handset are usually the first to gain knowledge of the emergency and rush to the scene. It is after they have been to the scene of the emergency to assess the situation that the doctor is alerted – if needs be.

As in the case of the GP practice in the community, GP consultation is by way of a prior appointment. Inmates wishing to see the doctor have to complete a form and present it to healthcare. They may be given the next available appointment or be placed on the waiting list. Provision is made for emergency cases through the embargos.

Generally, inmates do not have to wait long for the opportunity to see a GP. I will venture to say that, based on my experience, they seem to have lesser waiting times than in the community! Still, I have been to some prisons where inmates have complained of having to wait a long time for the opportunity to see a doctor.

37) CLINICS WITH STOPWATCHES ATTACHED

As in the community, appointments are usually based on ten-minute slots. One or two slots in both the morning and afternoon clinics are usually blocked, or earmarked, to make room for emergencies.

As in a GP practice in the community, there are usually two sessions, morning and afternoon, each lasting between three and three and half hours. The morning slots usually last from 08:30am to 11:30am; the afternoon clinic is usually from 1:30pm to 4:30pm.

In the community, one can walk freely to one's GP clinic. As might be expected, this is generally not the case in the prison setting. Usually, inmates are issued with movement slips a day prior to their appointment. These are permits that allow them to move from their cells to healthcare. In the case of Category C and Category D prisons, movement is unrestricted. Put another way, inmates are generally permitted to walk the distance from their cell to healthcare unaccompanied.

In Cat B prisons, the whole group of prisoners needing treatment on a particular day are moved in a group accompanied by officers into the waiting room. After their treatment they are escorted back to their cells.

The situation is different with Cat A prisoners. They are usually moved in smaller groups into the consulting room. Before they are permitted to go to the treatment room, they are subjected to metal detection.

As I mentioned earlier, vulnerable prisoners are not allowed to mix with the general prison population even when it comes to healthcare appointments.

The same applies to patients on the Segregation Wing, who are seen by the doctor three times in the week. In case their condition requires them to be examined within the confines of the doctor's consulting room, they are usually placed either first or last on the doctor's list.

Some prison healthcare units boast hospital-type wards where inmates whose conditions do not warrant admission to hospital yet require regular if not constant observation by healthcare staff are kept.

As I mentioned earlier, the daily prison routine follows a strict regime. The healthcare appointments are adjusted to fit into this strict regime.

The clinic should be over at a set time and cannot usually be prolonged. Patients who are not seen within the period are rebooked for a later period. There are instances, though rare, when the whole day's clinic has had to be cancelled at short notice, usually for security reasons.

One day when I arrived to work at a high security prison, the nurse escorting me turned to me and said:

"You have chosen a favourable day to work!"

"What do you mean by that?"

"Well, at least, as far as the morning clinic is concerned, you will have very little to do."

"Why so?"

"Well, there is a general lockdown. There is a suspicion of firearms in the prison. Specially trained personnel have been called in. They are undertaking a cell-by-cell search."

Do you recall, reader, the morning you woke up as a child to be told that the school day had been cancelled for whatever reasons? What feeling went through you – delight?

That was exactly the feeling that went through me on hearing the news!

38) "DRUGGIES" AND THE RECEPTION DOCTOR'S NIGHTMARE

S o far I've described the situation of a normal GP clinic, a clinic involving inmates already in prison. I will now turn my attention to the reception clinic.

New admissions to a prison, whether they are on transfer from a different prison, or whether they have arrived direct from court – sentenced or remanded – have to go through a registration process, usually referred to as reception screening. The first part of the process is undertaken by the prison officers.

Next, they are screened by a nurse or healthcare assistant. Newly arrived inmates without any medical condition needing a doctor's attention are escorted by officers to the various wings of the prison.

New arrivals requiring immediate doctor's attention are referred to the reception GP.

Whereas the routine GP clinic is held during the morning and afternoon, the reception clinic is held in the evening and usually lasts from 6pm till around 9pm in most prisons.

In some remand prisons boasting large prison populations, the reception clinic could last till somewhere around 10pm. My longest reception clinic lasted till around midnight. On that occasion, I was working in a London prison boasting a large prison number. Usually, the clinic ended around 10pm. The instance I am referring to happened at the climax of the riots that engulfed the UK in the summer of 2011.

New inmates came pouring in till around midnight. I was even asked to stay on beyond midnight! "No way", I objected, "I was officially booked till 10pm. I have used my discretion to help till midnight. Any new receptions needing medical attention might just as well be sent to the A&E!" As an agency doctor not bound by the contract of the prison, I could stand my grounds. I might even have been obliged to stay on till daybreak, had I been an official employee of the prison!

There are usually two categories of new arrivals needing the doctor's attention. The first group can be subdivided into two: those on regular medication in the community, who need to be re-prescribed by the prison doctor; and those wishing to be prescribed something for a medical condition that has cropped up at short notice, for example headache, stomach upset, nausea and vomiting, etc.

Prison rules dictate that inmates arriving in the prison are not permitted to continue on their repeat prescriptions until they have been prescribed or re-prescribed by the prison doctor.

Usually, new inmates have to surrender all their items, including their medication – in whatever form they are – to the reception officers. The officers in turn pass them on to the reception nurse, who in turn passes them on to the reception doctor.

Another general rule is that whatever medication the inmate was on in the community needs to be confirmed with their GP practice/surgery before it is re-issued by the prison doctor.

Thus, even if inmates arrive in the prison with packs of their present unexpired medication, neatly labelled in their names, the doctor usually is not permitted to continue them until they have been confirmed.

The practice is for prisoners who are on medication in the community to sign a consent form to permit the prison to request confirmation of their medication from their GP practice. The form is then faxed to the surgery. Usually, GP practices respond quickly to such requests; in case of delay, the healthcare administration usually chases them up.

Where the medications are for medical conditions such as diabetes, high blood pressure, epilepsy, etc., where interruption of therapy even for a short period of time is not desirable, the reception doctor usually prescribes for a few days pending confirmation by the community GP.

Even after their medication has been confirmed, the medication they surrendered on their arrival is not returned to them but disposed of. (The rule is for inmates to take only medication prescribed and dispensed by prison healthcare personnel.)

The second category of inmates requiring urgent medical attention on arrival in prison includes those we usually refer to as the "druggies".

Quite a good proportion of new inmates arriving in prisons are addicted to one, two, three or even more of substances such as alcohol, heroin, cocaine, cannabis, diazepam, amphetamine, etc.

They are usually arrested for shoplifting, theft, burglary, etc. They may spend a night or two at the police station before being sent to prison. If the police station has access to a police doctor, they are prescribed something to mitigate withdrawal symptoms. Some of them may be on methadone substitution in the community. In that case, the officer may collect the day's dose to be administered under the supervision of a member of the healthcare personnel.

The scenario just described is the ideal case scenario. From my experience, many inmates addicted to the named substances usually arrive at the reception clinic displaying various degrees of withdrawal symptoms. This is especially true of new arrivals to the Monday evening reception clinic. Some of them will have been arrested on Saturday or Sunday and will have spent the weekend in police cells without adequate treatment for their addiction.

There have been a few instances when inmates heavily dependent on alcohol have displayed quite severe withdrawal symptoms at the reception clinic. If the prison happens to boast a hospital-like ward of the type described above, they are sent there for close medical observation until their condition permits them to be discharged back to the normal wing. Where the prison has no such facility, such new arrivals are sent to the A&E.

New arrivals to prison addicted to one or more substances of addiction have to undergo a detoxification regime for the substance involved. Currently there are detoxification and/or substitution programmes for the following: alcohol, diazepam as well as opiate-based medication such as heroin, methadone and buprenorphin (subutex).

For the sake of readers not familiar with the term *detoxification*, I shall provide a short explanation.

In the strictest sense, detoxification is a medically supervised treatment program for those addicted to alcohol and various drugs and designed to purge the body of the intoxicating or addictive substances. In prison, it has the goal of preventing prisoners from developing withdrawal symptoms related to the abused substance especially during the initial stages of their stay.

Depending on the substance of abuse involved, prisons may embark on a detoxification or substitution regime.

Those addicted to alcohol are put on a detoxification regime involving chlordiazepoxide (also known as librium) or diazepam for a period usually lasting between a week and two weeks to prevent them from developing alcohol withdrawal symptoms.

Those addicted to diazepam are started on an initially high dose, which takes into consideration the extent of their addiction. The starting dose is gradually reduced over several days till they are completely weaned off it.

Those addicted to heroin, whether by way of smoking, injection or both, are placed on an initial dose of methadone. The dose is titrated upwards till stabilisation has been achieved.

New inmates who are on methadone or buprenorphine-substitution therapy in the community are usually maintained on their usual dosage after confirmation by their respective community drug teams.

Talking of methadone ... it assumes such importance within the healthcare unit of a prison, in particular in the case of remand prisons, that it will be a disservice vis-à-vis its special position in prison medicine not to dedicate a chapter to it.

I will therefore return to the issue of "King Methadone of Prison Medicine" at a later stage in my narration.

39) BARELY IN PRISON, RUSHED TO HOSPITAL

Inmates are expected to be fit for prison. That is usually the case. The majority arrive in relative good health, if not perfect health – indeed in a state of health that generally permits them to serve their sentences.

There have been a few instances, however, when new arrivals have been sent straight to the A&E.

It could be that the medical condition warranting attention developed suddenly whilst being transported from court to the prison. It could also be that the offender had been discharged from hospital to prison and that the condition that necessitated the admission had worsened whilst being sent to prison. When that happens, the reception doctor – or if there happens to be no doctor around, the lead nurse – calls the ambulance to get the inmate to the A&E.

If after treatment the A&E doctors deem him or her fit to return to prison, he or she may be returned that very night – otherwise he/she stays in hospital until they are fit for discharge back to the prison.

40) INMATES WITH QUESTIONABLE SANITY

Q uite a large proportion of prison inmates have mental health issues of various manifestations. I read the other day a report to the effect that nine out of ten prison inmates display a degree of mental health problems.

Recently, there was talk of the mental health personnel being sent to police cells to assess offenders regarding their state of mental health before being sent to prison. Based on my personal experience, I find it a good move. Indeed, I have in not a few instances seen inmates in the reception clinic who were in a state of mind that led me to question the fairness of the criminal justice system vis-à-vis this category of inmates. Though not a specialist in the field of psychiatry, my common sense alone has been sufficient to help me conclude that the individual concerned deserved to be on a psychiatrist ward and not in a prison. Indeed, on not a few occasions I have asked myself these questions:

- Did this individual understand the charge levelled against him/her by the judge?
- Is this individual even aware of the place he/she has been sent to?

Even if they have been sent on remand pending the hearing of their case in court, to be fair to them, prison is the last place they should be sent. Society, instead of helping them overcome their mental impairment, is punishing them for their mental condition by sending them to prison!

I remember an instance when an inmate in a mental health home was sent to prison for assaulting a member of the healthcare staff!! Much as I pity the victim of such an assault, it is difficult to comprehend why someone who – to put it bluntly – has lost his/her mind should be held accountable for his or her actions!

An extreme case of mental derangement I have come across in my prison work involved a prisoner in his early 20s sentenced for the attempted murder of his mother through strangulation. He had stated that a voice had urged him to strangle his mother with whom he lived alone. The first psychiatrist asked to assess his mental state came to the conclusion that he was not mentally sound to stand trial. The prosecution, not happy with the conclusion of the expert, demanded a second opinion.

There is a saying, "two doctors, three opinions." In the end the second expert contradicted the conclusion of the first. Eventually, the court followed the advice of the second expert.

I wish those who sent him to prison were given the opportunity to follow up the case in prison!

Throughout the six months he was in prison he lived in a literal nightmare! Indeed, he remained in an almost permanent state of mental derangement. The situation manifested itself among others in aggression and violence towards prison staff. In an almost permanent state of agitation, he tended to hit anyone or anything that came his way. After almost six months of terrorising everyone who came his way, the prison authorities finally decided to transfer him to a high security mental health hospital.

The above example no doubt represents an extreme condition. Usually, inmates with mental health problems are managed not only by the GP but also the Mental Health Inreach Team (MHIT), which is charged with identifying and treating mental health disorders among prisoners in England and Wales.

During a reception screening, inmates with mental health issues are referred to the GP or the MHIT or both. The MHIT after reviewing the notes may decide to get involved or may leave it to the GP to prescribe medication. The MHIT may eventually get a psychiatrist involved.

Before I leave this area, I'd like to state that the healthcare team, GP, nurses and the MHIT are not the only support services available in the prison for MH issues.

Other support systems available for those with mental health and other emotional problems may involve the following:

- Listeners
- Chaplaincy
- Samaritans' Phone
- Officers

41) WELCOME TO THE PRISON PHARMACY

When one consults a doctor in the community one is usually given a prescription. Whatever happens to the prescription, whether the individual concerned takes it to the chemist/pharmacist to get it dispensed, whether the individual takes only part of the medication and disposes of the rest, whether, as in the case of certain medication with potential for abuse, the medication is sold to those addicted to them on the street, the prescriber is usually left in the dark as to what happens to the medication prescribed.

The situation is different in the prison setting. Prisons go to great lengths to ensure the medication prescribed is not only taken but also that it is not abused, traded, or hoarded with the possible intention of overdosing on it.

I will now touch on the various steps in place to ensure medication safety in prisons.

RISK ASSESSMENT: Before they may be considered to keep their own medication, prisoners are risk assessed based on a score system for their suitability to do so. Factors taken into consideration include previous history of self-harm, drug overdose, medication trading, passing on medication to others, etc.

Those found suitable for keeping their current medication are made to sign a contract that lays down the conditions under which the medication is issued. Failure to comply with the requirements –

concealing or trading the in-possession dispensing – could lead to the privilege of keeping their medication being revoked.

The maximum period for which inmates are allowed to keep medication in their possession is usually 28 days. The right is granted to those who are deemed to be at low risk of doing anything untoward with their medication.

Some may be deemed fit to keep their medication, but not up to the maximum period of 28 days usually allowed. For this group of inmates, medication is issued on a weekly basis.

Patients on the ACCT are generally refused in-possession medication.

CLASSIFICATION OF MEDICATION: Apart from risk assessment, the prison healthcare uses the system of medication classification to reduce the risk of medication abuse, trading, overdose, etc.

Under this system, prison medications are grouped into three categories:

i)   those that are dispensed strictly supervised;
ii) those that are usually dispensed supervised;
iii) those that are generally dispensed unsupervised.

i) Strictly supervised medication is not dispensed to patients for keeps under any circumstances. Instead they are always dispensed directly to the patient, to be swallowed or drunk in the presence of the dispensing healthcare staff. Medications that fall into this category are strong pain killers such as morphine and antipsychotic drugs such as haloperidol and risperidone.

ii) Medication usually dispensed supervised include antidepressants and opiate-based painkillers such as tramadol and dihydrocodeine. Such medication could be issued on a daily, weekly or even monthly basis to inmates based on the outcome of their risk assessment.

iii) Medication generally dispensed unsupervised constitutes medication with practically no potential to addiction and which can hardly cause harm to body, even in case of overdose. Examples are antibiotics and medication prescribed for abdominal conditions such as indigestion, acid reflux, constipation, etc.

UNSUPERVISED MEDICATION: Unsupervised medication may be dispensed on a daily, weekly or monthly basis. In the case of drugs prescribed as "daily in possession", the inmates are required to queue up once in the morning to collect the dosage meant for the day.

If the medication concerned is issued as "weekly in possession" the inmate queues up once every week to collect the week's stock.

Finally, inmates line up once every month to collect medication issued monthly in possession.

To check for compliance and also to ensure drugs are not being hoarded or passed on, prisons regularly carry out surprise audits on those prescribed in-possession medication. Based on the time that has elapsed since the medication was dispensed, the prisoners are expected to provide a stock to tally with the amount of tablets still remaining on them. Those who fail a medication audit usually have their right to keep unsupervised medication revoked.

SUPERVISED PRESCRIPTIONS: Inmates queue once, twice or three times daily as the case may be for their supervised medication. Supervised prescriptions are usually dispensed following a stringent regime. The prisoners line up at a window to the pharmacy, under the watchful eyes of one or more prison officers.

When it gets to their turn, they are first asked to open their mouths wide to be inspected by the dispenser to ensure nothing is concealed there.

Next, the medication involved is handed to the inmate – in the case of a tablet or a capsule, it is placed in their hands. They are then asked to put it in the mouth. Next, they are handed a plastic cup containing water and asked to swallow the tablet with its help.

As a final step in the ritual surrounding the dispensing of supervised medication, the inmate is required to open his/her mouth widely for inspection by the dispenser.

Those unfamiliar with the extent to which prison inmates may go in their effort to conceal medication in their mouths, usually with the goal to passing it on to others, may wonder why such detailed dispensing rituals are necessary. To show how necessary precautions are, I shall give a few examples of some of the bizarre tricks or methods by which inmates seek to conceal medication they are supposed to drink or swallow.

Buprenorphin (subutex) is one of the highly sought-after drugs among prison inmates with opiate addiction problems. Together with methadone, they form the main substitution drugs for opiates addicts. Usually, it is dispensed in a sublingual form, which means the patient has to allow it to dissolve under the tongue before swallowing. Inmates bent on passing such drugs on to others do their best to conceal them under the tongue. Even though they are required to drink water and open their mouths for inspection, some still manage to outwit the nursing staff and pass on their medication to others.

Some prisons, in their attempt to overcome the problem of drug concealment, turn to liquid forms of the medication concerned if available.

42) KING METHADONE OF JUNKIELAND

As I mentioned earlier, it would be a disservice to the special position methadone occupies in prison medicine not to dedicate a chapter to look at it in some detail. So here we go…

For those not familiar with it, methadone is a synthetic drug that is similar to morphine in its effect but less sedative and is used as a substitute drug in the treatment of morphine and heroin addiction.

The goal of placing heroin addicts on methadone is to help reduce their craving for heroin, and in the end help them overcome their heroin addiction.

If the insight I have gained interviewing prison inmates I have seen in the reception clinic over a period of more than a decade is anything to go by, I am beginning to think the goal of putting addicts on methadone, with the hope of getting them off heroin, is a futile exercise. At best, it may help reduce the quantity of heroin they consume daily, but to get them to quit heroin is well-nigh impossible. Indeed, my impression is that about 80 per cent, if not more, of those in the methadone-substitution program are still topping it up with heroin – injected, smoked, or both!

For many a prison inmate methadone may well be regarded as second in importance only to oxygen, far ahead even of food and water in their scale of preference! As I mentioned earlier, when inmates addicted to heroin arrive in prison, especially if they happen to have spent a few days at the police station, they tend to display initial signs of withdrawal. In such situations, they are more concerned about their methadone than even about food or their other prescribed medication.

Indeed hardly have they taken their seat beside the doctor's desk in the consulting room than they will ask:

"Doc, when am I getting my methadone?"

"Well it is my duty to prescribe; the dispensing will be done on the wing."

"Today?"

"I hope so."

"Doc, please, do ensure that I get it!"

When an inmate arrives in prison and claims to be on methadone in the community, we first test his/her urine for the substance.

Even if they test positive to the substance, that does not lead us to believe they were indeed on a prescription in the community – they could even have been buying it illicitly. So we contact either the dispensing chemist or their community drug team for confirmation.

The situation is simple for all parties involved – the inmate, the reception doctor as well as the dispensing nurse – if the prison healthcare team manage to get hold of the prescribing community drug team or the dispensing chemist/ pharmacy on the phone to confirm the new arrivals' methadone prescription. The prescribing doctor is even more at ease if the community prescription happens to be supervised prescription. In such cases, the inmates have to drink the day's prescription in front of the pharmacy staff.

Things become a bit complicated if it involves unsupervised prescriptions, where the addict is usually dispensed methadone to take home. Some collect it on a daily bases, some weekly. How can one, in such a situation, be certain that the methadone that has been collected is also consumed by the individual concerned and not passed on to other addicts!

To be on the safer side, therefore, those on unsupervised prescriptions are usually placed on a small dose that is titrated upwards till attainment of stabilisation – just as in the case of those smoking or injecting heroin.

While there are tablet forms of methadone, methadone is generally administered in the liquid form to opioid addicts – both in the community and also in prison. The reader may consider this unimaginable; it is, however, true that in some instances, prisoners go to the extent of attempting or even indeed actually succeeding in passing on methadone given to them as a drink to others! One might wonder how this could happen. Why would anyone want to pass on a liquid poured into the mouth to others? Some may find it disgusting, beyond belief – yet it is true: somehow inmates are able to outwit the nursing staff by feigning swallowing! They then rush quickly to spit everything out and pass it on to the inmate who is keen to swallow it!

Methadone is usually supplied to the prison on a daily basis. It occupies such an important place in the life of an addict that, should something happen to prevent it from being delivered to inmates on a particular day, it may well spark off a riot – a serious one for that matter.

43) THOSE WHO SEEK CAPITAL OUT OF THEIR DOCTOR'S PRESCRIPTION

U sually when a patient visits a doctor in the community with common back pain, the doctor is likely to prescribe what is usually known as *non-steroidal anti-inflammatory* drugs such as ibuprofen, naproxen, diclofenac or simple pain killers such as paracetamol. Strangely, what can be described as standard therapy in the community, doesn't seem to work for a good number of prison inmates.

As I mentioned earlier, quite a substantial proportion of prison inmates are addicted to heroin either through smoking, injection or both. Some may be former heroin addicts who, prior to their imprisonment, were on methadone or subutex-substitution programs in the community. When such individuals arrive in prison, they are put on either methadone or subutex. Where they are serving short sentences, they are usually maintained on doses of methadone or subutex sufficient to stabilise them and see them through their sentences.

In regard to those serving medium and long-term sentences, it is usually the policy of prisons to attempt a gradual reduction with the goal of stopping the prescription in the course of their imprisonment.

It is the members of this group of inmates who pose a great challenge to the doctor in regard to opiate-based prescription medication. Whether they are on methadone or subutex, whether they have been weaned off the above medication, inmates in this group tend to display an ongoing yearning for opiate-based medication.

How do they get them prescribed? By feigning symptoms. In this regard, the most common symptoms feigned involve some form of back pain; in particular lower back pain. Aware of their aim of getting prescriptions for opiate-based medication at the back of their minds, one can easily understand why they are not keen to accept non-steroidal anti-inflammatory drugs such as ibuprofen and naproxen for pain relief.

This leads me to the matter of tradable (highly sought-after) prescription drugs in prison.

The first group of the medication involved consists of opiate-based medication. Opiates are substances that act on so-called opioid receptors in the brain. In its natural originality, opioids are found in the resin of the opium poppy plant. Examples of naturally occurring opiates are opium, morphine, and codeine. The most common effect of medicinal opiates is pain relief. There are semi-synthetic and synthetic versions of opiates; examples are heroin, methadone, buprenorphine, dihydrocodeine, tramadol and oxycodone.

Next to consider are gabapentin and pregabalin. Both are licensed among others for the treatment of some types of epilepsy as well as for the treatment of neuropathic pain and anxiety. For readers who are not well-versed in medical matters, it will suffice to know that neuropathic pain is a complex, chronic pain state that usually results from damage to the nerve fibres themselves, the damaged nerve fibres sending incorrect signals to other pain centres of the body. In other words, the nerves, which usually transmit impulses from various organs to the brain, will, in the case of neuropathic pain, be sending wrong information generated within themselves to the brain.

When I started working in UK prisons about a decade ago, both substances were not among the frequently prescribed group of medication in prison. The situation is different now. There is now clearly a big rise in the use of pregabalin and gabapentin in prisons – both prescribed and illicitly obtained.

Many inmates will have already started on these forms of medication in the community. Once these are confirmed by the community GPs on their arrival in prison, the prison doctor is usually obliged to continue the prescription. Failure to do so could lead to intervention by the inmates' solicitors.

Those who do not arrive in the prison on such medication, in the course of their stay, try to feign their symptoms to obtain the drug either for personal use or to trade it further.

This is particularly the case if they happen to carry surgical scars from previous surgeries – never mind if such surgeries were performed several years if not decades ago. It is as if they all undergo the same coaching in the symptoms that could be feigned to get these drugs prescribed, for those seeking them usually present the following symptoms:

- numbness and tingling in the feet or hands
- feelings of pins and needles
- burning, stabbing or shooting pains in affected areas.

"I was injured in a road traffic accident several years ago; it led to nerve damage which in turn is causing feelings of pins and needles in the affected part of my body. Doc – I suspect nerve damage."

I would reply: "I too underwent surgery to one of my legs several years ago. I am not experiencing any 'pins and needles'!"

"Well, doc, everyone is different; I do indeed experience excruciating pain especially at night, which keeps me awake! Believe me, I am not one of those who comes here to feign symptoms to get medication; no, I am genuinely in agony, so please help me!"

* * *

Other highly sought-after drugs are those classified as benzodiazepines. The benzodiazepines belong to a group of medicines that are used to treat anxiety, nervousness, tension, sleeping problems, etc., by slowing down the central nervous system. Examples include diazepam, lorazepam and temazepam, chlordiazepoxide and nitrazepam.

As I mentioned previously there is a culture of poly-drug use in the community. Many who are addicted to heroin are also addicted to diazepam. Many cite the internet as their source of supply.

On their arrival in prison those who claim addiction to diazepam and who test positive to it, undergo gradually detoxification. Apart from the purpose of detoxification of those addicted to alcohol or diazepam itself, prescription for diazepam and other benzodiazepines is highly restricted in the prison. Usually those who have been taking them for a long period are taking them for various mental health conditions. Such prescriptions are usually initiated by a psychiatrist.

Readers will recall I cited this group of medication as falling under the category of medication prescribed as *strictly supervised*. To prevent concealment for whatever reason, many prisons resort to liquid versions only. Notwithstanding such precautions, the benzodiazepines, especially diazepam, manage to find their way into the prison to be traded and abused

* * *

The next group of drugs to mention are the so-called Z-drugs. These are referred to as Z-drugs because the names of most of the drugs in this category start with the letter Z – Zaleplone, Zolpidem, Zopiclone, etc. Also referred to as 'sleepers', they are used in the treatment of insomnia or the inability to sleep.

The complaints of sleep disturbance or the inability to sleep are so widespread among prison inmates that strict prescribing guidelines are in place in most prisons I have worked in to control or regulate the prescription of drugs used for these complaints. Usually, unless the prescription is initiated by a psychiatrist (in which case they could be for long-term use) they are usually prescribed for short-term use, usually for up to three nights.

* * *

Before leaving this field, I will turn my attention to another drug that is gradually gaining popularity among prison inmates, namely mirtazapine. It is meant to treat depression, obsessive- compulsive disorder (OCD) and a range of anxiety disorders. Though it is not normally prescribed for those complaining of an inability to sleep, it has a sedative effect on those who take it. The sedative effect – actually a side-effect – of the medication has led to its popularity among prisoners. As I have mentioned, the prescription of pure sleeping tablets, such as the

Z-drugs, are restricted in the prison setting. To get their hands on these – and especially the popular mirtazapine – inmates consulted complain of feeling anxious and depressed. Those who are already on different types of antidepressants will tell the doctor they are not working, eager to try something else.

Those who are yet to be prescribed any antidepressant are likely to tell the doctor someone he or she knows has reported a marked improvement in his/her symptoms since that individual began taking mirtazapine, so they should also be prescribed the same. If the doctor replies that mirtazapine is not the first line of therapy, the inmate may still plead that he or she should be started on the medication straight away. If the doctor remains adamant, the inmate may agree to try what the doctor thinks best until the next review. The inmate may not wait for the scheduled review, but turn up a few days later complaining of terrible side-effects from the medication prescribed.

"Why don't you try me on mirtazapine instead, doc? I took a few tablets prescribed for a different inmate and it worked wonders!"

"You are not supposed to take medication prescribed for others!"

"I know, doc! Nevertheless, please prescribe it for me to prevent me from taking that desperate step."

It may not be the best practice; I must admit though that in some cases, I do give in and prescribe the medication as requested.

44) SWEET OR BITTER, THEY SWALLOW THEM ALL!

I have made a peculiar observation in regard to some prison inmates, especially those addicted to drugs: they have the tendency to take any drugs they can lay their hands on! Even if the drug is prescribed for a condition they do not have, they are happy to take it if offered to them by fellow inmates!

On one occasion I nearly got myself into trouble as a result of the peculiar behaviour or attitude of prison inmates. How did it happen? I was interrupted during my consultation by a nurse who came to request a methadone prescription for a patient. The prescription was due on that very day and needed to be done without delay. I promised to do it immediately after I had finished seeing the patient I was attending to. In the end, a mix-up occurred. I recorded the name of the patient I had just seen on the chart instead of the person for which the prescription was meant.

Later in the day the patient was escorted by a prison officer to collect the methadone. One might have expected him to make it clear to the officer he was not on methadone. But no! He readily accepted and drank the medicine in front of the nurse.

As he later admitted, he accepted it because he wanted to test it since many others he knew were on it! Happily the dose was not high enough to cause any problems. He was sent to the hospital wing to be observed overnight and discharged the next day without any complications.

45) DOCTOR PARACETAMOL!

This is a note of warning for the GP booked to work in a UK prison for the first time. Please be aware of the kind of prisoners you can expect!

Indeed, unlike the situation in the community where one can generally assume that the patient's story or complaint is genuine, the prison setting can be fraught with deceptions and subterfuge on the part of the patient.

Some of the patients are decent citizens who might have ended up in prison for offences such as exceeding the speed limit or non-payment of council tax. One would expect this group of individuals to seek medical attention only when really needed – that, from my experience, is generally the case. On the other end of the spectrum are inmates who are not to be trusted for any word that issues from their mouth! Those who fall into this latter category are those addicted to various substances, especially those with heroin addiction. They will go to any length to fake their symptoms to acquire prescriptions for highly sought-after medication such as tramadol, dihydrocodeine, or pregabalin.

Word of mouth spreads quickly among prison inmates. This is true also concerning the arrival of a new doctor in a prison. Prisoners have the tendency to make appointments to see the new doctor to test his or her resolve in regard to his or her prescribing habits.

Is the new doctor generous in his/her prescribing habit? Can he/she easily be persuaded to prescribe DFs (Dihydrocodeine), Gabi (Gabapentin), Pregab (Pregabalin)?

Aware of this, some prison healthcare departments choose to assign a member of the healthcare staff to new doctors over the first few days, to assist them in the clinic by alerting them beforehand about patients on the list for the day who are known for their drug-seeking behaviour.

I was assisted in the same manner during my early days as a prison doctor. In the course of time, I developed a kind of "no-nonsense" attitude towards the "drug-seekers". Instead of the much-coveted tramadol, dihydrocodeine, pregabalin, etc., I would issue medication such as ibuprofen, naproxen, paracetamol – much to the displeasure of those feigning "excruciating back pain". In the end, some ended up calling me names like "Dr Ibuprofen"; "Dr Paracetamol", etc.

46) THE PRISON
DOCTOR'S DILEMMA

O ne may well say that the problem of drug abuse has literally been relocated from the community into the prison setting. Caught in the middle is the prison doctor. A balancing act is required.

There was a colleague who adopted a very extreme position, determined not to prescribe any opiate-based medication. Not only that, she went to the extent of stopping the prescriptions of those who were already on such medication. As might be expected, her attitude was not well received by those affected.

As their frustration and anger mounted they not only bombarded the healthcare administration with complaints but threatened legal action. Not only that, some threatened to instigate protests. To avoid further escalation of the situation, the prison refused to book her for further sessions.

In some respects my colleague was right for, to be honest, only a small proportion of inmates I have come across in prison on opiate-based medication actually deserve them for the management of their pain. Indeed, for the great majority of them, their pain could be controlled just as well by NSAIDs (non steroidal anti-inflammatory drugs) like ibuprofen, naproxen, diclofenac , etc.

The dilemma faced by the prison GP is not helped by his GP colleagues in the community. I base my assertion on my personal observation made in regard to frequent offenders – mainly drug addicts who serve short sentences for various petty crimes, released into the community only to return to prison after a short while. On their arrival in prison, a GP may refuse to continue their prescription for opiate-based medication initiated in the community. Even if such prescriptions are continued initially, they may be stopped after a while. The inmates concerned are released from prison after a short stay only to return a few weeks later with prescriptions for even higher doses of the opiate-based medication concerned! Let the reception doctor dare refuse to prescribe and he or she will be threatened with legal action by the upset prisoner!

I will cite a few examples to illustrate the kind of dilemma facing the prison doctor when it comes to the prescription of some forms of the medication under the category referred to above.

A female prisoner who had been complaining of ongoing low back pain which was apparently not being relieved by the maximum doses of both pregabaline and dihydrocodeine was referred to the pain clinic for review. The pain management consultant recommended that pregabalin be stopped since she was already on dihydrocodeine. In line with that advice, the prison doctor gradually reduced and eventually stopped the prescription of pregabalin. Not happy with the situation, the patient complained to a solicitor. The solicitor contacted the healthcare administration on the matter. The healthcare administration on their part referred her back to the prison doctor. I was deputising for the regular doctor who happened to be on leave so the onus fell on me to decide on the matter.

How did anyone expect a visiting GP, deputising for the regular doctor, to reverse the decision of the regular doctor taken on the advice of a consultant? Nevertheless, I could not summarily dismiss her request without reason. I had, as it were, to find a way, to *cover my back*. I realised that my clinical findings alone would probably not convince the solicitor. Happily, she had had a recent MRI scan of her back that showed normal findings. Referring to my normal clinical findings supported by the results of the MRI, I refused to put her back on pregabalin.

As might be expected, she was not convinced with my decision, threatening to involve her solicitor.

On another occasion, a patient was directed to my clinic for a second opinion in regard to her pain management. After she had been caught concealing her prescribed dihydrocodeine – the reader will recall that it belongs to the group of opiates – the regular doctor stopped it. For the management of her (presumed or alleged) pain, the doctor prescribed paracetamol and ibuprofen – but she refused to visit the medical hatch to collect the new prescription.

One might consider the matter closed; but no! Due to her complaint to the healthcare administration accompanied by the threat of solicitor intervention, she was given the opportunity to consult a different doctor for a second opinion on the matter. That different doctor happened to be me.

Equipped with the stated background information, I decided to take particular note of how she walked into the consulting room. She did indeed walk briskly into the room, with no indication of being in pain.

"How can I help you today?" I began after she had taken her seat beside the consulting desk.

"My prescription for dihydrocodeine was stopped by Dr D. without any apparent reason. Since then my back pain is really killing me; indeed, I am in real agony!" she began.

"Wait a moment, Miss. I saw you walking into the room. You walked here freely – not the way a person who is 'in real agony' with back pain walks!"

"That is not right, doc, I *am* in excruciating pain; indeed, I am in agony, my back pain is killing me!"

"Well, I'm not convinced. You are currently on ibuprofen. If it is not helping, I am happy to change it to naproxen."

"I want my dihydrocodeine back; otherwise I will get my solicitor involved!"

"Well, you are free to do so. Just as I cannot dictate to your solicitor in matters of law, in the same way I do not expect your solicitor to dictate to me regarding matters of medical practice!"

"You are really rude to me!" she protested. "I have never met any doctor who is so rude! I want my dihydrocodeine back!"

"Well", I said with forbearance, "I think your medical condition does not warrant the prescription of dihydrocodeine. If you are not happy with my decision, I will ask admin to arrange for you to see another doctor – for a third opinion!"

"You **** off, rude doctor!"

Saying that, she charged out of the room, banging the door loudly behind her as she left.

47) TRUST BUT VERIFY!

Whatever the case, healthcare personnel, especially doctors, are advised to adhere strictly to the principle of trust but verify when working in the prison setting; failure to do so might land the doctor in trouble – as the following case demonstrates:

3/07/13: A prisoner in his mid-20s began a six-week sentence in prison in the south of the country. He mentioned on his arrival in prison that he had been diagnosed with colon cancer. He refused any further investigation or treatment, citing his short sentence of six weeks as the grounds for his stance.

18/07/13: The patient was transferred to a prison located about 100 miles to the north of the first prison where I was working. He reported his recent diagnosis of colon cancer to the reception doctor. As in the case of his previous prison, he refused the doctor's request to be referred for surgical assessment and possible surgery. Apart from the reason of his short sentence, he also mentioned his objection to having to carry a colostomy bag in the event of surgery as the grounds for his refusal of surgical intervention. The reception doctor duly documented his warning concerning the health implications of his decision.

22/07/13. The following entry was made in his records: "Patient complaining of gradual intensifying of his abdominal pain despite being on a highest dose of tramadol." In response to that oramorph (morphine), a more potent opiate-based pain killer, was prescribed to be dispensed when required.

26/07/13: "Patient still complaining of excruciating pain; requesting more frequent use of oramorph."

28/07/13: One of the leading nurses, in response to the patient's frequent request for oramorph, made an entry in the patient's records to the effect that there was no medical report on file to confirm the diagnosis of the alleged colon cancer.

29/07/13: In the course of the day, with the consent of the patient, an urgent request was sent to his community GP for information regarding the alleged diagnosis of colon cancer. Not long thereafter his GP faxed his medical records through.

It confirmed a colonoscopy (a test that allows the doctor with the help of a thin, flexible tube called a colonoscope to look at the inner lining of the large intestine) was performed on 8/03/13. In the process a biopsy (an examination of tissue removed from a living body to discover the presence, cause, or extent of a diseased tissue) was carried out with the following outcome: No evidence of inflammatory bowel disease or malignity (cancer)!!

When confronted with the report from his GP surgery, the patient was still adamant on having being diagnosed with colon cancer. As a result of the information received from his GP, the prescription for tramadol and oramorph was stopped immediately.

48) ADDICTED TO PRISON

After reading through all that I have written so far concerning the daily hassle one is subjected to at the prison gate, the security clearance procedure, the key talk, the abuse, insults and, in some instances, physical confrontation with inmates, one might be inclined to ask – why did you choose to subject yourself to all that over a period of more than ten years when you could just as well have found a job as a GP in the community?

It will be hypocritical on my part to state here that I was motivated purely by an idealistic premise expressed by the question: "If you don't go to treat the inmates locked up there, who else will?"

Whereas that thinking might have been a factor, I must admit that personal interest played a more decisive role.

Due to a medical condition afflicting a family member, I may at any time have to interrupt my work for an undetermined period to attend to the needs of the family. Thus I sought a job that would give me the needed flexibility to enable me to attend to family matters at short notice.

In taking that into consideration, I decided against a salaried job bound by a contract.

In the end I settled for the role of self-employed GP. I did not set up my own practice but instead registered with various agencies looking for doctors to fill short-term vacancies in GP practices.

Initially the agencies were sending me to work in both community GP practices as well as in the healthcare departments of various UK prisons.

In time, probably as a result of the experience I had gained from working in prisons and also the fact that prison work is not every GPs favourite cup of tea, the agencies literally overwhelmed me with prison jobs.

On my part, in time, despite the challenging prison environment, I seemed to have developed some kind of *addiction* to prison work!!

Did some of the factors I am about to touch upon contribute to this curious state of affairs?

Unlike the situation pertaining in several other countries where a paediatrician (a doctor specialising in the treatment of children) in the community is the first point of call for sick infants and children, in the UK a GP is assigned that role in the community. While not having any aversion towards children, in particular sick children, I prefer dealing with adult patients.

Usually in the case of an adult patient the doctor has only one individual to deal with. As might be expected, children usually seek the doctor's help in the company of their parents, either one or both of them. I have nothing against that. There are instances, though, when the accompanying adults by their behaviour lead the doctor to wonder as to which of the two parties, the infants/children or the adults accompanying them, deserve medical attention. Working as a prison doctor, I am spared that scenario.

An agency GP sent to work at a prison usually works seven to eight hours with a short break of about half an hour. On the other hand, if I am booked to work in a GP surgery in the community, I usually work three hours in the morning, followed by a two-hour unpaid break and finally a three-hour afternoon session. Thus at the end of the day, I usually earn more money working in the prison on a particular day than I would do working in the community.

The paradox of working as a prison doctor is that, though one is exposed to more dangerous patients than in the community, the actual workload is usually not as heavy as in the community. There is a tendency, for various reasons, for many an inmate to decline, at the last minute, to attend their GP appointments. Especially during the afternoon, there could be a non-attendance of up to 30 per cent or more.

A prison lockdown, for whatever reason, could also lead to the cancellation of the GP clinic at short notice.

It is superfluous to mention here that I am paid for my attendance – whether inmates attend their clinic or not.

49) THOSE WHO SPEND THEIR LAST PENNY ON DRUGS RATHER THAN THE DENTIST

Most prisons have dental clinics. The waiting list for the prison dentist is usually long. This is especially the case in remand prisons. Several reasons, including the following, account for the situation.

A good proportion of inmates for various reasons arrive in the prison with dental problems.

Some of them have no fixed address in the community, a fact that makes it difficult if not impossible to register with a GP or dentist.

Even if they are registered with a dentist, drug addicts may prefer using their money for drugs rather than risk spending money in a dental clinic and so avoid making appointments at a dental clinic.

Prior to their arrest some inmates might have been on the run from the police, a fact that might have dissuaded them from accessing the community dental facilities for fear of being arrested.

I had an opportunity to share thoughts with the dentist in one of the prisons with a population of around 1,000 inmates.

"The prisoners keep on complaining about the long waiting list", I began.

"Well, we are doing our best. When they were in the community they hardly found time to visit the dentist. The moment they arrive in prison, however, they want to be seen by the dentist straight away!"

"In the community, they are probably more occupied with how to source their drugs than find time to seek a dental appointment!"

"There was an instance when we started a treatment procedure. It could not be completed prior to the prisoner's release. We urged him to contact his dentist in the community to complete it. He returned about six months later – nothing had been undertaken."

50) IN CHAINS TO HOSPITAL APPOINTMENTS

ROUTINE GP REFERRAL: Prison inmates are promised the same level of healthcare as their counterparts in the community. In the foregoing chapters I described a normal GP surgery.

Hardly any prison has a resident consultant.

Some prisons have arrangements with consultants who visit on a regular basis. This is generally the case regarding psychiatrists. Indeed, almost every prison I have been to has a visiting consultant psychiatrist who attends on quite a regular basis – not surprising, considering that mental health issues are quite widespread.

The rule however is for prison GPs, just like their counterparts in the community, to refer cases needing consultant review to the nearest consultant available.

FAST-TRACK REFERRAL: As in the community, inmates suspected of cancer are referred by way of the fast-track referral regime that requires such patients to be seen within a period of two weeks. If the doctor suspects cancer, the fast-track transfer pattern applies.

Some prisons have their own in-house x-ray and ultrasound machine. As for more sophisticated devices, I have never seen any in the prisons I have worked in. For those prisons without x-ray and ultrasound devices, as well as for all investigations requiring the use of MRI, CT, echocardiography and other sophisticated devices, the GP has to refer inmates to the nearest available hospital.

Unlike the situation in the community, inmates are not sent appointments directly; rather such appointments are sent through the prison healthcare administration. Indeed, it is strictly forbidden for inmates to know the exact dates of their hospital appointments. One might wonder why. I am told it is to prevent them from possibly organising an escape attempt, for example by way of an ambush. If, for whatever reason, a prisoner gets to know the date of an impending hospital appointment, the appointment is cancelled and re-scheduled.

There have been instances when their GPs have referred them to consultants in the community. The letter goes to their home address. Their relatives then send it to them in the prison. They in turn, after reading it, present it to the doctor.

If the appointment is for a hospital far away, the inmate is referred to a local hospital. Even if the appointment is for a local hospital, it has to be re-arranged, once the inmate has had knowledge of the appointment date.

There have been instances when inmates have taken up an outside appointment, when the unsuspecting consultant or his/her secretary has revealed the date of the next appointment to the prisoner concerned. Even if the prison officers do not mention it to hospital staff in the presence of the prisoner, they will surely pass the information on to healthcare administration to request them to contact the hospital to re-arrange the appointment.

From time to time routine hospital appointments have had to be cancelled, sometimes at the last minute for various reasons:

i)   The patient may just simply refuse to attend!
ii) There may be not enough officers on duty to escort the inmate.
iii) It could also be due to intelligence that has reached security pointing to a possible escape/kidnap plot.
iv) The officers earmarked for that particular escort duty have had to be re-assigned to escort an inmate requiring more urgent hospital treatment. (One might ask – why not transport both inmates in the same vehicle? That was how I reasoned initially. For security reasons it is not permitted, I was told.)

Transport for a routine examination, as might be expected, comes with an element of surprise to inmates. I remember a consultation I had with an inmate one morning. He was quite upset that an investigation he had been promised several weeks before had still not taken place.

"I'm reaching the point where I'm considering involving my solicitor!" he threatened.

"Be patient", I advised. "We are doing our best. You should bear in mind that those in the community also have to wait for their GP appointments."

"But I have been waiting for months!"

"Very well, I'll look into this for you."

I clicked on the electronic file where such appointments are stored. Lo and behold, he had an appointment that very day, in the afternoon – barely three hours from the meeting!

"Doc, any good news?"

"I told you to be patient!"

"Do I have an appointment?"

"Yes indeed!"

"When approximately? I know you cannot mention the exact date and time."

"It won't be long, my friend."

"Sure?"

"Sure!"

If appointment dates are revealed only at the last minute, what about investigations requiring a degree of preparation on the part of the patient, for example colonoscopy? A key requirement for a successful outcome of such a procedure requires the patient emptying the contents of the bowel a day prior to the investigation. To achieve this, the patient is required, on the afternoon or evening before the procedure, to drink a liquid that will trigger bowel-clearing diarrhoea. If the prison happens to boast a hospital wing, the inmate is sent there a day prior to the investigation to prepare for the procedure. If that is not the case, he or she is left in his/her usual locations and given the fluid to drink without going into detail as to when exactly the investigation is due.

It is superfluous to mention that inmates are not left alone to attend their hospital appointments. Depending on their security classification, they are accompanied by at least two officers. For those classified with the most dangerous prisoners around, they may be accompanied by as many as six officers.

They are not only escorted, they are handcuffed to one of the officers. My understanding is that even during the procedure, ultrasound, echocardiogram, colonoscopy, etc., they still remain handcuffed throughout their treatment, no matter how intimate the examinations or procedures may be.

Usually, before they leave for such a procedure, a doctor or other healthcare personnel signs a paper to indicate under what circumstances such restraining may be relaxed. Usually, it is only in case of general anaesthesia that the lifting of the restraint is permitted.

Some prisoners, perhaps as a result of the embarrassment of attending their outpatient hospital appointments in chains, are reluctant, and may even refuse to attend.

There was a case when a patient, adamantly refused to attend. He preferred whatever the consequences might be, even death, to going to hospital. In the end we had no option other than to request him to sign a disclaimer to that effect.

In recent times, telemedicine consultation is resorted to whenever appropriate.

Just prior to their departure to hospital, a healthcare personnel competent to do so signs a paper to indicate the inmates are fit to attend the appointment. On their return to prison a doctor or a nurse has to sign another paper to the effect that they are fit to be kept in prison.

Just as in the case of transport to prison for outpatient appointments, when it comes to hospital admission, officers keep around-the-clock watch. For Category B, C and D prisoners, this usually involves two officers at a time.

In case of high security prisons, four officers are usually involved. In cases involving exceptionally dangerous prisoners, up to six prison officers may be employed to keep guard.

As I mentioned earlier on, a few prisons boast hospital-like wards where prisoners whose conditions do not require hospital treatment, but are deemed to be of the nature that requires regular monitoring, are kept.

Occasionally, inmates on admission to hospital, after they have recovered sufficiently, are not discharged straight back to the wing, but rather to the hospital ward. Nurses observe them around the clock.

51) IN CASE OF EMERGENCY CALL "999"!

In the previous chapter I described routine hospital appointments. What happens in cases of emergencies such as heart attack, unconscious inmates being cut down from ligatures in attempted hangings, life-threatening injuries, etc.?

In response to such emergencies, a code red or blue alert is usually triggered over the prison radio system.

Healthcare personnel, prison officers and ancillary staff, as the case may be, rush to the assistance of the sick person or victim to administer first aid, including cardiopulmonary resuscitation (CPR) if required.

Based on the condition of the patient, the lead nurse or GP as the case may be instructs the prison gate to call the 999 emergency number without delay.

From my experience, with the exception of prisons located in remote areas, the response of the ambulance is usually swift, comparable with the response time in the rest of the community.

Hardly anyone enters a prison without going through some kind of security check. The ambulance, yes even the flashing blue-lighted ambulance, is no exception. As might be expected, however, the check in this case is simplified to save precious time.

Just as in the case of the community, paramedics, after attending to a patient, may decide to take the patient to hospital for further medical attention. As one might deduce from my narration so far, they can only transport the patient under the escort of prison officers.

On some occasions, disagreements may develop between healthcare and the prison officers in regard to hospital transfer.

On one side is the doctor representing healthcare who is of the opinion that an inmate needs to be seen at the A&E. On the other hand is the governor who is faced with the problem of shortage of prison officers to escort the prisoner (every prisoner transport to the community is accompanied by at least two officers) – this is particularly the case during the night and on weekends.

In a few cases, the duty governor intervenes, either by way of the telephone or by appearing personally to discuss the matter. Can the condition of the patient being sent to the A&E permit waiting till the next day? It is usually a matter of clinical judgement. If it involves, for example, sending someone with a suspected fracture of a finger, then the matter could indeed be left till the next day.

Much as I may sympathise with the position of the governor, if the condition of the patient is life-threatening and makes it absolutely necessary for him or her to be sent for treatment – for instance a patient with a suspected heart attack, or one who is asthmatic and suffers from severely impaired breathing, or is an assault victim suspected of internal bleeding – then I stand my grounds on the matter and leave it to the prison to provide the necessary security to facilitate the transport even if it requires recalling officers from their night or weekend rest.

52) THE CLOCK TICKING TO THE FINAL END BEHIND PRISON WALLS

What do we do with terminally ill inmates?

I have in mind the case of a 43-year-old lady. Midway through her sentence, she began to report occasional coughing up of blood. She was also treated for a recurring chest infection. A routine chest x-ray request was made in response to her condition. It showed suspicious lesions in the right half of her lungs. The doctor requested further investigation in the form of a CT. Then, just as she was awaiting an appointment – it happened! She was found in her cell in a very bad state "literally swimming in a pool of blood she had coughed up".

She was rushed to hospital. The CT scan confirmed the spread of cancer to various parts of her body. Initially it was difficult to make out the source of the primary cancer – Uterus? Ovary? Further investigation revealed it was in fact a primary cancer of the lung.

She had given a history of smoking: according to the records she had given up smoking a few months previously.

After spending a few days in hospital she was transferred back to jail. The plan was to initiate chemotherapy – which would involve her being sent to the outpatients of the local hospital.

I was the first doctor to see her on her return from hospital. Her poor state of health was enough to melt a heart made of stone. Common humanity, dear reader!

Though she was quite alert and engaging, her breathing difficulty was obvious. The problem was exacerbated by the fact that she was not coping with the hard prison mattress and pleaded for a softer mattress.

Next, she requested something to help her sleep. Usually sleeping tablets were not encouraged. In this case, however, I prescribed for her without any hesitation.

As I have said, some prisons boast hospital-like wards. This was not the case in this particular prison. It was a nightmare, not only for healthcare officers but for prison officers as well. The medication she was prescribed included those that required to be dispensed at night. For that to happen, adjustment needed to be made to the prison routine. Furthermore, extra staff both from healthcare as well as prison officers, needed to be sent there to supervise the dispensing.

Eventually the lady was transferred to a special unit where the sentencing conditions were quite relaxed and beds more comfortable.

There are provisions in the UK criminal justice system that allows inmates like the one I have just referred to, who fulfil certain criteria, to be considered for early release on compassionate grounds. As one senior colleague, a medical consultant, who has worked in the Prison Service even longer than me told me, there are so many barriers built into the provision, hardly anyone fulfils them in practice.

"In more than a dozen cases I have been involved in over the years, only one of such applicants has had the application for early release granted. All the others were left to die in prison!" he told me.

PART THREE
NOTABLE CASES RECALLED

In this section I shall narrate a few of the numerous personal experiences I have had, as well as stories and cases I have come across in my work as a prison doctor.

I shall reproduce some of the cases/stories here, not so much with the goal of making capital out of other people's suffering, but in the hope that they will serve as deterrents to others, especially the young reader for whom much of life's journey still lies ahead.

One indeed has to exercise care and caution in life, for any small mishap, or failings, could lead to trouble, trouble that could eventually lead to a spell behind bars.

53) LEFT TO FREEZE IN THE COLD

Once when I turned up at the gate of a prison for women where I had worked before on a weekly basis over a period of about two months, I expected to be allowed in without much ado. That was not the case.

This particular prison had a large wooden gate that was kept locked from the inside at all times.

On arrival, the visitor has to ring a bell. The gate keeper would then open a small window built into the door to attend to the visitor.

One has to produce an ID. In the case of a visitor like me who was not a permanent staff member, the gatekeeper then goes through a pile of sheets affixed to a clipboard in his hand to check whether the visitor is expected. After checking that the visitor is indeed on the list, he or she opens the gate to let the visitor in.

It was a chilly, rainy day in December and forecasters had predicted rain for most of the day. Indeed over the last few days it had rained heavily in several parts of the UK, leading in some parts to flooding.

Since, as I mentioned, I had been working there on a weekly basis for a while, I thought I would be let in quickly, especially in view of the inclement weather.

Moments after ringing the bell I heard the sound of the unlocking of the locking device of the window. Soon a strongly built gentleman in uniform, whose age I put at around 35, appeared at the window.

"How can I help you?"

"I'm the doctor for the day, sir!"

"Your ID please!"

That was the question I was expecting, so I had already pulled my ID out of my pocket. Without uttering a word, I handed it to him.

"Wait a moment while I check through my papers."

Saying that, he began, one after the other, to check through about a dozen sheets fixed to a clipboard in his hands.

"Your arrival has not been announced by healthcare", he said after a while.

"I'm a regular here, sir! I was here last week."

"Well, sorry about that, sir, I have to follow protocol. I have to first check with healthcare."

"How long will that take?" Indeed it was a superfluous question. I had worked in the prison long enough to know it could take a few minutes to several.

"About five minute, sir!"

"Please hurry up – it's wet and cold here!"

"I'll do my best."

Saying that, he shut the window and left me alone at the mercy of the elements.

I did not remain alone for long. Before long a well-dressed gentleman in his mid-40s walked up to the gate. He was better prepared for the wet weather, for he was carrying an umbrella.

"Good day, sir", he greeted me and took his position behind me.

"Sir, you need to ring the bell to draw their attention; I'm already being attended to."

Not long after he had rung the bell, the gatekeeper arrived.

"How can I help you?"

"Legal visit!" he replied.

"Your ID please."

As in my case, he went through the sheets on the clipboard.

"Any mobile phones?"

"No, sir!"

"Then come in, sir."

"Hope you have not forgotten me!" I inquired, just as he was about to shut the gate in front of me.

"No, sir, we are still checking with healthcare. I'll attend to you as soon as we hear from them."

Soaked and shivering, I was left alone for another few minutes.

Just as I was about to ring the doorbell again to remind them I was still outside, I could hear the sound of someone releasing the locking mechanism of the window. Not long thereafter, the gatekeeper appeared at the gate.

"I must disappoint you, sir, at least for a while", he began, with no emotion in his face.

"What is the matter?"

"Unfortunately, your gate pass has expired. Healthcare failed to renew it. We have urged them to file a new application!"

"How long will that take?

"Five to ten minutes, perhaps longer. It all depends on how quickly healthcare submits the paperwork."

Was it exasperation; was it frustration that filled me?

"Well, I cannot wait here any longer. I'll go back to the car park and wait in my car."

"That's a good idea. I suggest you come back after ten minutes to check."

When I returned after about ten minutes, I met a different officer – the other one had probably ended his shift.

"Your ID please?" he said after opening the window in response to the sound of the doorbell.

He clearly had been briefed about my case, so opened the door for me without asking any further questions.

Waiting for me in the large open space in front of the reception was the healthcare manager herself.

"Sorry, doc, for the inconveniences!" she began. "The gate pass I applied for you expired yesterday. I should have submitted one for the week beginning today."

"Why don't they issue a gate pass valid for the remainder of my time here?"

"Well, that's only possible after you've been given a key talk for this prison."

Without any further comment, I headed for the reception and presented my ID. Shortly thereafter my visitor's ID was issued.

As I walked beside the healthcare manager on the approximately 500 yards walk to the healthcare building, there was silence to begin with. As we were about halfway along the distance of our walk, she turned to me and said: "We seem to be treating you unfairly whenever you visit us. Today we left you standing in the rain. Not long ago we left you sitting in the waiting room of the reception for almost an hour!"

"Indeed! On that occasion I nearly dozed off as I waited for ages to be collected!" was my reply.

54) PRISON SEARCH GONE WILD

One day I was posted to work in a private Cat C prison. I was asked to be searched. The search was conducted very thoroughly, by a lady who was young enough to be my daughter. I was used to searches, but this one was unusually thorough. Not only was a body search done, but my bag was also thoroughly searched. It felt as though I was under suspicion.

As a result of this I decided henceforth to leave all my items in my car, with the exception of two pens and my ID. I even left my stethoscope behind, having established that there were a couple in the doctor's office.

Nothing happened on Monday, Tuesday and Wednesday...

Then came Thursday morning.

On all the previous occasions, I had gone through a routine check at the gate. Not so on this occasion. This time I was asked to undergo what they described as an enhanced check.

The check would not take place downstairs but rather on the first floor. I was told that I was not being singled out and that everyone had to undergo that level of check occasionally. In the end I got the all clear to proceed to healthcare to start the assignment for the day. The morning clinic was unusually busy that day.

There was an hour break between the morning and afternoon clinic. I took the opportunity to head for the prison canteen to satisfy my hunger.

In the majority of prisons I have worked, the prison canteen, indeed, if there happens to be one, is usually located within the walls of the prison. The situation was different in this particular prison. Contrary to what I was used to, they had their canteen or mess on the outside, about 100 yards from the main gate.

After I had finished my meal, I went to my vehicle to make some calls. After about half an hour I made my way back into the prison. When I reached the gate, I was expecting them to return my visitor's pass, which I had to leave behind, and allow me back into the prison. Not so!

"We want to conduct a search on you", the woman officer said.

"What!" I exclaimed. I could not believe I had heard properly.

"We want to search you."

"But, I just left here for the canteen. I did not drive away. I have remained within the premises of the prison."

"Please, you have to oblige."

For the first time since I started working in the prison more than six years earlier, I felt I had had enough. I wouldn't allow myself to be humiliated.

"No, I refuse to be searched", I replied boldly.

At that juncture, she called her superior.

"Either you allow yourself to be searched or we walk you to the gate!"

I wondered if the officer was even slightly aware of the amount of work that was accumulating in the healthcare wing. The clinic list for that afternoon was considerable. Beside that there was a mountain of paperwork that needed to be attended to.

"No, I refuse to be searched; please hand me back my ID so I can leave for home."

She might have thought it was an empty threat, but I was determined. I had been booked to work the whole week and I had worked for three and a half days. I had earned enough money to sustain me and my family.

Soon I was heading for the hotel I had booked into for the week. (If I am booked to work in a prison far from home, I stay in a hotel or guest house during the week and leave for home at the end of the week.)

"I need to go back home", I told the receptionist.

"But I thought you were staying till Friday?" she inquired

"I have to leave early; please prepare the invoice to cover the four nights, as booked."

Just as I had finished packing my items and was getting ready to dial the agency that sent me to work there to report the matter to them, my phone rang – the call happened to be from the very person I was about to call!

"The prison has called to report you have left them! Tell me what went wrong?"

I narrated my part of the story.

"Healthcare needs you to do their prescriptions. They are also struggling to find cover for tomorrow."

"I am sorry; I refuse to return to that prison, not only today, but indefinitely. They better ask the officer at the gate to do the prescriptions for them!"

55) THE WALLET THAT EVAPORATED INTO THIN AIR!

I used to take my wallet with me to prison – no longer!

During consultations I hang my coat behind my chair. One after the other I call the patients in. There is not a moment when I leave any patient alone in the room – which in any case is not allowed for security reasons.

On one occasion I was diligently going about my duties when one of the prison officers entered the room.

"Doc, have you lost anything?"

"Not that I can think of."

"Well, I found this wallet with your personal belongings in the corridor, not far from here!"

"That just can't be true! It was in my coat when I hung it on the chair."

"Well, doc, you have to be more careful. Remember you are in prison. Do please check to make sure you have not lost anything", he advised as he handed the wallet over to me.

I checked it, as advised. Everything was intact, with the exception of a £20 note I had taken along (usually one is not allowed to take anything above that amount into prison).

Clearly, one of the patients had snatched the wallet from my pocket as I was concentrating on the job of documenting.

But how did he manage it, since the wallet was in the pocket of my coat that hung on the chair on which I was sitting and never left? I was indeed working with professional pick pockets!

Not long thereafter I was studying my consultation notes when the inmate I was seeing interrupted me.

"Doc, you should be careful with your wallet!" he warned, pointing to the wallet in one of the pockets of my coat. "Before you know it, someone will have grasped it!"

"Thanks for your advice!" I said.

Since that day I decided not to carry my purse into the prison but rather keep it safely hidden inside my car. Mind you, someone warned me that was also not safe since there had been a few break-ins in the visitors' car park. Well, it seems I was caught between a rock and a hard place! In the end I decided the "hide in car" strategy was the best option. I have been doing that for over five years now and so far things have gone well.

56) THE PRISONER WHO THREATENED ME DIRECTLY

When one begins to work in a prison, one of the first things a doctor's attention is drawn to is the alarm buzzer. We are told to press it whenever in danger.

There was only one occasion when I pressed it – to summon assistance when during a consultation a prisoner turned violent. Apart from that single instance, I never resorted to pressing the buzzer. There were occasions when, in retrospect, I might have summoned help – but on the whole I managed to handle precarious situations on my own. Whether I was right to do so, I do not know.

Thinking back to one occasion when I resisted pressing the buzzer and dealt with the situation myself: when the patient arrived, I was my usual self – I greeted him politely. The aggressive manner in which he began to speak to me immediately alerted me to the fact that this individual was not going to be an easy nut to crack! The trouble began when we discussed his medication. He wanted to continue the medication that was quite popular in prison and I made him understand that I could not prescribe it until it had been confirmed by his GP. That did not go well with him.

"I need my meds! I need them for pain relief!" he insisted.

"Well, I'm prepared to prescribe common painkillers like paracetamol. The others need to be confirmed by your GP before they can be prescribed."

"I don't want any f**** paracetamol or ibuprofen! I want my medication now!"

"Unfortunately, that cannot happen…"

"What a **** doctor!"

"Friend, you need to mind your language!"

"You **** doctor!" he screamed, and raised his arms in a threatening manner.

That was the moment when I should have pressed the buzzer and waited for help – but my human instinct took over and told me to try and engage him myself. A disinterested observer might say that was not the best approach. However I decided to take control of the situation since he was not a strongly built fellow – his threats could thus at best be interpreted as empty ones.

I noticed he looked around for an object to use as a weapon, but there was nothing around. So instead of pressing on the buzzer, I confronted him and ordered him to leave the room. This caused him to raise his arm as if to give me a blow to the face. My response was to do likewise, as if to let him believe I would return an "eye for an eye!" Seeing this, he made for the door, still yelling and cursing at the top of his voice. I followed him into the corridor and reported him to an officer. He was then whisked away.

Of course he did not get what he wanted though I did my duty by completing a form that is usually faxed to his GP the following day. Normally he was required to sign it but the circumstances did not favour this routine procedure!

A few days later I returned to work in the prison and, out of curiosity, I went through his notes to follow up on him. I was surprised to read that on the very night of his arrival, he was found with a self-inflicted injury to his left wrist. At the time he was found, he had already lost a good deal of blood. He was sent to A&E.

Why did he self-harm himself? He was protesting at the fact that he had not been given his medication!

57) MY COLLEGUE WHO
WAS SPAT AT!

I have experienced abuse, insult and verbal assault during my over ten years work in prison.Indeed, there have been instances when I left my consulting room to urge the prison officers to come over and forcefully remove a patient from the room.

So far such aggression of prisoners towards me has been limited to verbal assault; indeed, I have on a few instances been told to f*** off!

When something of this nature happens, the doctor can open an incident form, which can eventually result in disciplinary action being taken against the perpetrator.

Others have threatened me with legal action on grounds of negligence, dereliction of duty of care, etc.

Fortunately, I have so far been spared any form of physical assault, such as being spat at. A few other colleagues however have not been that fortunate, as the incident described below illustrates.

Due to a backlog of work, a prison that normally ran a single-doctor GP clinic, engaged another doctor and myself to run the morning clinic on a particular day.

I held my clinic on the ground floor whereas my colleague had his on the first floor. Midway through the clinic, I heard a commotion above me. Moments later the alarm bell sounded. Soon I could hear sounds of footsteps rushing upstairs.

After my patient had left the room, I came out to establish what the matter was.

"It involved your colleague", I was informed. "He had a confrontation with the patient." Later I learnt the details: it involved a prisoner who was known for his violence. On several occasions, the regular GP had refused his request to prescribe pregabalin. If only the matter could have been laid to rest at that point – but no, upon the prisoner's insistence of his rights for a second opinion, he had been booked in to see the visiting doctor.

Aware of his violent disposition, the prison took the precaution of posting an officer in the room.

As might be expected, on seeing the new doctor he repeated his request for pregabalin.

After examining him, the visiting doctor came to a similar conclusion as the first doctor and refused to prescribe the medication. A few exchanges followed as the doctor tried to explain the reason for his decision. It was when the doctor took his eyes off the patient and directed his attention to his computer that it happened! In a twinkling of an eye, just as the doctor began to write his notes the patient stood up suddenly, bent his head towards the doctor and spat in his face! Below is the actual description of the incident by the colleague concerned:

"At that point he lunged towards me and spat in my face. The spit fell on my glasses and also part of my face. I was quite shocked, but the prison officer was quick in restraining him. The inmate was attempting to pick up the weighing scales on the floor, presumably to throw them at me, but again was prevented by the prison officer. The officer urged me to press the alarm button. In the chaos, I found it and pressed it. The next thing I heard was the height-measuring stand crashing towards the desk and I assumed the prisoner may have thrown that towards me."

After some initial difficulty, the officer managed to restraint the strongly built prisoner. Moments later more than half a dozen officers, responding to the alarm, rushed in to finally defuse the situation.

58) OVERDOSE CASE IN WHICH I WAS INVOLVED

Once while on reception duty I saw a patient with mental health issues. The nursing staff had already confirmed his medication with his GP practice. It was the policy of the prison to prescribe such medication as supervised. It could be changed to weekly in-possession later on, subject to the outcome of the risk assessment.

I followed the prison policy and prescribed it as supervised for a period of 28 days. The prison involved was a large Victorian prison with an average inmate population of over 1,200. Usually, three doctors were on duty during weekdays. There was a doctor on Saturdays. The prison used the services of the on-call doctor service on Sundays.

During the weekdays, one of three doctors was assigned the role of duty doctor. The duty doctor did not usually have a regular clinic. Instead he/she saw emergency cases of the day and also issued repeat prescriptions.

On Saturdays, there was no regular clinic; the duty doctor saw emergency cases, issued repeat prescriptions and saw new inmates requiring the doctor's attention.

There was a healthcare station on each of the several wings of the prison. The practice was for nurses of the various wings to gather the prescription charts that needed to be renewed on their respective wings and bring them to the attention of the duty doctor. The requests were usually delivered by them, sorted into two piles – supervised and non-supervised.

It is expected of a doctor signing a prescription to check for prescription error; in other words, to check its accuracy, both for the clinical indication and also the dosage involved.

In the prison setting, the doctor has another responsibility, which is spared his colleague in the community – namely, to check that an inmate being prescribed non-supervised medication has also been risk assessed and found suitable for in-possession medication.

The matter is straightforward if it involves a prescription being initiated by the doctor. He/she can verify from the records to ascertain if a risk assessment has already been done. If it turns out that it hasn't, he/she could carry on the assessment if time permits. Where this is not possible due to time constraints, I usually prescribe as non-supervised and request the nursing staff to carry out the risk assessment at a future date.

The situation was not that clear cut for the duty doctor in the prison in question, and he was asked to re-write a pile of prescription charts presented by nursing staff from various wings of the prison.

As I indicated above, the charts were sorted into two different piles – supervised and non-supervised prescriptions.

Owing to the large number of inmates in that prison and the limited time at the disposal of the doctor, it was practically impossible for the doctor to verify every single unsupervised prescription request to ascertain whether indeed the inmate in question had been risk assessed. Instead one was left to trust the good judgement of the nurse who carried out the sorting.

I worked on a regular basis, on average about three times weekly, for a period of about a year. Eventually, my work there came to an end.

Several months after I had stopped working there, I was contacted one day by the prison through my agency. I was asked to write a statement in regard to a patient I had seen during my time there. In due course further details of the matter came to light.

The patient had overdosed on his prescribed medication – at a time when I was no longer working in that prison! He was rushed to hospital. After spending some time in hospital, which included a few days on the intensive care unit(ICU), he was discharged back to the prison. He had sued the prison for compensation.

I was involved in the matter because, as it turned out, I was the first doctor to change his prescription from supervised to weekly in-possession, giving him the opportunity to hoard his medication, which he then took all at once with suicidal intent. As I said, I happened to be the first doctor to see him. I had rightly prescribed his medication as supervised. Looking through his records, it was clear I was the first doctor to change the prescription from supervised to non-supervised some time later!

The point of contention was – on what basis did I do that, for no risk assessment had been recorded in his records.

Noting the date of the prescription shed further light on the matter – it was done on a Saturday. If that was the case, then it was done at a time when I was the duty doctor. I had not seen the patient directly. I had as usual been presented with a pile of charts that needed to be re-prescribed – as usual grouped into supervised and non-supervised.

Though I had checked the accuracy of the doses of the various medications, I had in good faith thought the nurses who presented the charts had done a diligent preliminary job. As it turned out, in this particular instance, that was not the case.

Though the prisoner had survived his suicide attempt without any lasting damage to his health, he was suing the prison for compensation on the grounds of medical negligence and breach of duty of care.

The claim was directed not only against the prison but also the individual staff members directly involved in the chain of events that led to the incident.

After a legal tussle that lasted a few months, he was finally awarded £25,000 compensation. The prison had in the course of the proceedings assumed full responsibility for the matter and relieved individual staff members involved in the case from culpability.

59) CHEATING ON A WIFE THAT LED TO PRISON

E ducational facilities abound in the prison. Indeed those serious and committed to self-improvement can turn a bad situation around. I have in mind an inmate who turned up in my consulting room with several folders in his hand.

"Are you doing your PhD?" I joked.

"You're not far wrong! I'm preparing for my final exams. I'm just returning from Education [lectures]."

"Really?"

"Yes."

"What are you studying?"

"Law."

"Indeed?"

"Yes, you heard me right. Well, doc, I'm by no means a typical prisoner, not a druggie; not a fraudster, not a ... well, to be honest, I'm in prison because of my personal moral failings."

"What happened?"

He hesitated a moment.

"You don't have to tell me anything", I reassured him.

"No, doc, I will let you know. Initially, I had difficulty speaking about it. It is however a while ago so I am able to speak about it. It is a mistake I committed in my relationship that brought me to this situation. I cheated on my wife. Everything went well for a while, I think about two years. Then my mistress wanted me to commit to a financial venture. At first I refused. She kept pressurising me and still I held firm. When she realised that things were not going her way, she devised a plan – to frame me."

"One day I had returned from work and was relaxing with my family when we heard a knock on the door. I opened the door only to realise it was the police. They had come to arrest me for rape, they announced! You can imagine the reaction of my wife! During the trial that ensued, my mistress managed to convince the jury of my guilt. It led to a sentence of seven years. Initially I was really devastated. At a certain point I even considered suicide. Eventually, I found the strength to face the future. In the end, I resolved to make the best of a bad situation by enrolling in a course to study law. I'm almost through now – indeed, I'm just preparing for my final exams."

"That's an incredible story!" I applauded.

"I'm still doing all I can to win my wife back, though so far to no avail. I'm terribly sorry I ever began the affair. I miss my children."

Listening to him, I felt his candour, realising this man was deeply sorry for his infidelity and was genuinely repentant for what he had done and sincerely wished to return to his wife and children – though this was too late as he admitted.

60) THE DISCO BOUNCER ON A MANSLAUGHTER CHARGE

There's the case of a young, well-built man in his mid-20s I met in prison. He told me he was the "gatekeeper" or "bouncer" of a night club. He was doing his duty one night when a small group of young men turned up at the door bent on causing trouble. It was his duty to prevent them from entering. In the scuffle that ensued he punched one of them on the head. The man fell and hit his head on the hard concrete floor and he lost consciousness, never to regain it. A few days after the incident he was pronounced dead. At the time of our meeting the young man who had delivered the blow had just begun his sentence for manslaughter.

"I deeply regret what had happened", he told me. "I wish, indeed, I could reverse the clock of time! I would have gone about the matter differently. Now it's too late. I have to live with the fact of having taken someone's life for the rest of my life."

61) ALCOHOL THAT LED TO WIFE STABBING

I also have in mind the case of a middle-aged man serving a long prison term for manslaughter after being accused of killing his wife. According to him, both of them had alcohol problems. One day, under the influence of alcohol, they engaged in an argument over an issue that he admitted, under normal circumstances, should not have led to strife.

From his account, in the process of the argument, she made for the kitchen and threatened him with a kitchen knife – upon which he grabbed it from her and, in the heat of the moment, stabbed her to death.

He appeared to be very repentant, admitting to missing her dearly – and wishing that things had taken a different turn, indeed that she was still alive. Wishful thinking, since no amount of regret could recall her to life.

62) THE AFRICAN EX-GOVERNOR WHO KEPT THE "BANK OF AMERICA" IN HIS HOME

One day as I worked as the reception doctor, I was asked to see a middle-aged man of African descent. Nothing was extraordinary about him, apart from the fact that he told me he had been extradited from Dubai to face justice in the UK. He did not go into details and I also did not ask for them – after all I was there for his medical needs; the criminal aspect of his case was not an issue.

Another thing that struck me was the fact that he was on a quite expensive medication; usually we prescribed the generic equivalent of it in the cells.

The next day a female nurse from Nigeria approached me:

"Doc, do you know the person you saw yesterday?"

"No", was my reply.

"Well, he is the ex-governor of one of the southern states of Nigeria. He looted the state coffers empty. In fact he literally kept a bank in his home!"

"Really?"

"Well, if you want proof of this, just Google the story when you have a moment!"

Out of curiosity I did so on getting home and, lo and behold, I could hardly believe my eyes at the sight of piles, and piles of freshly printed US dollar notes stashed in his living room! It looked as if it was a warehouse of the US Treasury printing press! I do not think I can exonerate myself from the vice of greed, but what I saw that day made me realise I was rubbing shoulders with persons in a very different league!

The reaction of another Nigerian nurse reverberates in my memory: "That is embarrassing!"

Embarrassing indeed it was – when one considers the suffering of the masses of his own country. How indeed could any individual go to such lengths when his people are suffering from poverty and want? This thought was uppermost in my mind on the few occasions thereafter when I met him in the prison.

In the end he was jailed for 13 years after pleading guilty to embezzlement, fraud and laundering millions of British pounds.

About two years later I was working in a different prison when I saw his name on the list of patients to be seen on that day. He recognised me immediately.

"Why have you been moved from a lower to a higher category prison?" I asked.

"For my own protection", he said. "I applied to be transferred from London into a more remote prison for my own safety."

"But this place can literally be compared to the end of the world! Do you get visitors at all?"

"Of course I do! Even the high commissioner of my country visits me!"

"Indeed?"

"We are on very good terms!"

It is not up to me to pass judgement in the matter. I found it strange, nevertheless, that after looting huge sums of money from the coffers of his native country, the highest official representative of that country in the UK should find it necessary to travel the considerable distance to visit him in prison.

63) BURGLING FOR
BEDROOM TAX

T hen there was the case of a 25-year-old sentenced for burglary.
"You have to work hard to earn a living, my friend", I said.

"Thanks for your advice", he replied. "In the short term I found no way out."

"What happened?"

"I live with my mum in a three-bedroom house. We've been told to pay bedroom tax. Well, we couldn't afford it. We also did not want to vacate a home that we had become fond of. Threatened with eviction, I saw no way out of the situation other than to burgle another house to earn the money. The owner of the house happened to be at home and he raised the alarm and I was subsequently arrested. It was a really stupid decision on my part."

"What has happened to your mother and the house?"

"We have lost it; she has moved into a smaller accommodation."

64) AMERICAN BUSINESSMAN ARRESTED AT HEATHROW FOR UNPAID TAXES

It must be emphasised that all these accounts are from the point of view of the victims and must be taken with a pinch of salt.

Another story is one of an American businessman who claimed to be a multi-millionaire with business links to Latin America who found himself in unexpected trouble when he was arrested on his visit to the UK.

Certainly he did not anticipate what awaited him on his arrival at Heathrow airport. Instead of hiring a taxi from the airport to the luxury hotel he was booked into, he ended up in police custody and eventually in prison. Later it emerged that the arrest was in response to an international arrest warrant issued by the Netherlands, dating back several years.

He went on to state that he had run a business in the Netherlands several years before. He was wanted there for alleged tax evasion, something he vehemently disputed.

At the time of our meeting he was fervently fighting the threatened extradition to the Netherlands.

65) THE MYSTERY OF THE RAZOR BLADE STUCK IN THE EYE

How does a piece of broken razor blade find its way into someone's eye without the person noticing it? The scenario may be possible when one is a victim of a trauma. But then prison is not an ordinary place, where under normal circumstances one cannot imagine the impossible can take place and yet does!

Readers might recall the advert inviting injured prisoners to claim compensation. Perhaps that was the incentive for one inmate who suddenly began to complain of pain in the left eye.

On examination there was found to be slight redness of the eye. He was subsequently prescribed antibiotic drops for suspected eye infection.

That however brought little improvement and, after several days, he was referred to the eye clinic.

Initially even the eye clinic was at a loss as to what was behind the complaint. Then the reason came to light – a piece of a foreign body was discovered stuck in his eye!

Eventually, it was removed through surgery. The foreign body turned out to be a fragment of a broken razor blade!

"How did it get there?" the doctor wanted to know.

"Your guess is as good as mine!" was his reply.

Not long thereafter he was transferred from the London prison to the prison where I met him.

The vision in the affected eye was very impaired – indeed, the last consultation in the local eye clinic reported that he was in real danger of completely losing his sight in the affected eye.

When I saw him, he insisted that I document everything very carefully, for he was preparing a lawsuit against the prison for negligence.

When I returned to work in the prison several months later, I checked on his case out of curiosity. He had in the meantime been transferred to a different prison.

The last doctor's entry concerning his case stated that his vision had improved considerably. I asked myself how much compensation was awarded him!

66) SHEEP GRAZING PROBLEMS

O n one occasion an elderly man came to prison – on remand.
He appeared very embittered with the justice system. He was a
shepherd and had been sent to jail on breach of a court order in a case
involving him, his sheep and a neighbour, also a shepherd.

I am just reproducing his version of the matter. According to him
he was in almost permanent conflict with the neighbour. The conflict
centred on their respective grazing fields.

His neighbour had been accusing him of allowing his sheep to
wander and graze on his field – of trespass, you might say. All attempts
on his side to settle the issue amicably had proved futile. Instead his
opponent chose to bring the matter before a court of law. Eventually, the
court passed judgement based on the facts presented to it, prohibiting
his flock from trespassing onto the neighbour's field. In his view it was
a very harsh judgement. The court went into very precise details to lay
down the demarcation line or boundary the sheep were not permitted to
cross in degrees of longitude and latitude!

"Isn't that ridiculous, doc!" he exclaimed. "How can I teach my
sheep to understand that ruling?"

He was particularly exasperated about the judge's refusal to grant
his plea to spare him a custodial sentence. Instead he was made to serve
a short term – a few weeks – behind bars. His main concern while in
prison centred on his flock, which had been made to remain on the field
without their owner. As I listened to his case, I wondered whether his
sheep were keeping away from the neighbour's field now that their
shepherd was not around to direct them!

67) THE FEMALE PRISONER WHO JUST WANTED TO DIE!

I still remember the case of a female prisoner who had decided to end her life in response to a court decision to take her children into care. I had hardly taken my place in the doctor's office on my arrival to begin my Saturday duty when the code blue alarm sounded.

Soon I was running with all haste along the corridors following in the trail of about half a dozen staff members – officers and nurses. On our arrival, the scene that met our eyes was that of a lady of about 35 years of age surrounded by a couple of prison officers. They had in the meantime managed to untie the ligature she had tied around her neck with her bed sheet.

Her vital signs were checked and I was briefed about her case. News had reached her the previous day to the effect that the court had decided to send her children into care. Since then she had on several occasions tied a ligature around her neck. As a result she had been transferred from the normal wing to a special wing where each cell boasted 24/7 CCTV [closed circuit television].

After we had spent about 20 minutes trying in our various ways to speak words of encouragement to her and also calm her down, we left her and made our way back to the healthcare wing. Apart from the CCTV monitoring, an officer was posted at her door.

Barely had the officer taken her eyes off her when she jumped out of her bed, made for the WC in a corner of the cell, unloosed a metal hook fitted to it, and placed it in her mouth in an attempt to swallow it. In the process it got stuck in her throat and threatened to choke her.

I had just descended the two stairs leading to the ground floor on my way back to the doctor's office when the sound of the alarm filled the air again – "CODE BLUE, patient on the hospital wing!"

"Again?!" I said to myself. Soon I was running back to where I had just come from.

The scene that met my eyes was really desperate to say the least. She had turned really blue as a result of not being able to breathe. Those assembled – healthcare staff as well as officers – were striking her between the two shoulder blades in an attempt to dislodge the metal ring from her throat – in vain!

"Come on everyone, let's lift her up and turn her upside down!" one of the officers cried in desperation. With everyone present offering a helping hand we soon lifted her up, turning her upside down as we did so. Several desperate hits between her shoulder blades followed. Then it happened – to the relief of everyone present the metal ring dislodged itself from her throat and fell onto her bed!

"Hurrah!" we all cried with one voice.

The battle to save her was not over, however. She was still blue and not breathing! We then laid her on the bare floor and began CPR on her. Before long she began to breathe – though initially in an erratic manner. Gradually the blue pallor of her face changed to a healthy rosy hue.

Finally, she came back to herself. Her first cry on gaining consciousness was: "Please, leave me to die! I cannot exist without my children!"

I wish whoever passed judgement in her case had been around to witness the situation unfolding before our eyes!

Not long after she had come back to herself, the paramedics who had been alerted to the case arrived. Though her condition had improved significantly, they decided to err on the side of caution and take her to the A&E for further observation.

I did not return to work in that prison for a while. Usually, it is my custom to follow up on such extraordinary cases whenever I return to the prison concerned. On this particular occasion, however, I forgot to do so.

As I recount her case, I just wonder what became of her. Did she get her children back? Did the worst case scenario happen – indeed, did she eventually succeed in ending her life?

68) 20 YEARS, 36 PRISONS!!

Once a patient I consulted complained of anxiety and insomnia. "I am being released from prison next week; that has caused anxiety and lack of sleep."

"But you should be glad at the prospect of being released!"

"The whole family, my parents, my wife and two children will be meeting me – I'm really excited, especially in regard to my children... I have not seen them for almost 17 years."

"That's a really long time."

"Yes indeed."

"How long have you served?"

"20 years."

"For murder?"

"No. Theft, burglary and armed robbery. You know what? They did not keep me in one prison; instead they sent me all over the place. In all I have served in 36 different prisons spread all over the UK – England, Wales and even Scotland!"

At that juncture, he took a closer look at me.

"Doc, your face looks familiar to me. Have you worked in any other prison apart from this one?"

"Well, I've also been to several prisons spread all over the country. I sat down recently to count – I ended up with 45!"

"Surely, we must have met in one or more of those prisons! Indeed, the moment I entered the room, it struck me that I have met you before."

"Well, I do not recall you. Of course it is easier for my patients to recognise me than the other way round. I guess you have not served the full sentence; yes, that you are being released on licence?"

"Indeed yes, I have several years on my licence."

"Then you need to be a good boy in the community."

"Yes, I know – I need to behave and keep out of trouble, or they will send me straight back – in which case we may meet again!"

"Well, I will be glad to meet you again, but as a free man and not as a prisoner."

"I will do my best, sir."

"Promise?"

"Well, if you can trust the words of a criminal of my category, then, yes, I promise – on my honour!"

69) THE LIFE SENTENCE OF FATE

Inmates running away from the police may sustain various injuries in the process. These may include the following:

- They may be bitten by police dogs
- They may sustain fractures – to limbs, ribs, fingers, toes, etc., through various means – tripping and falling on level ground, falling from walls, jumping from various heights, etc.

When they are subsequently caught and/or arrested by the pursuing officers, the first port of call is usually the nearest A&E.

Depending on the injury involved, they may be treated and discharged into the custody of the law-enforcing officers; if the injury requires admission to hospital, they are kept under guard in hospital until such time that they are deemed fit for discharge.

Over the period I worked in prison, I saw on quite a regular basis, offenders who came to prison with casts on their limbs – both lower and upper – which were the result of injuries sustained in the manner already described. Some had to be given wheelchairs right from the outset, having sustained fractures to both legs whilst running away from the police.

Two particular cases are still fresh in my memory. One involved a 47-year-old lady who came to admission in a wheelchair due to the amputation of her left leg and chronic swelling and pain to the right leg, secondary to deep vein thrombosis (DVT), which in turn was the result of continuous injections of heroin into the great veins of the right groin. The left leg amputation was necessitated after, in her own words, she "jumped a fence and landed badly on my left while fleeing from the police. I shattered it badly in the process." She had not managed to overcome the main problem that led to her unfortunate situation – illicit drug use. According to her, since that first incident when she broke her leg, she had been going in and out of prison for drug-related offences.

Then there was the case of an inmate in his late 20s who jumped from the fourth floor balcony in an attempt to escape arrest and in the process sustained multiple fractures involving his pelvis and both lower limbs and arms – eventually leading to the amputation of his right leg. After spending several weeks in hospital where he underwent multiple surgeries, he was discharged back to prison to begin his sentence – and housed in the hospital wing of the prison in question.

The thought that came to mind when I saw him for the first time was: why wasn't he discharged into a residential home instead of a prison? Fate (or was it Destiny?) had as it were already imposed a life sentence on him. There was, in my opinion, no need to further burden the taxpayer with his imprisonment – in particular since his case did not involve murder, rape or terrorism.

70) THE UNUSUAL ALCOHOL SUBSTITUTE

The following conversation that I had with a prisoner aged about 60 years occupied my mind for a long time.

"What brought you to prison?" I wanted to know.

"Theft, doc, theft!" was the reply.

"What did you steal?"

"Alcohol!"

"Yes indeed?"

"Yes."

"Why did you do that?"

"You should know, doc!"

"What should I know?"

"That as a person addicted to alcohol, I need alcohol on a daily basis!"

"But that should not lead you to steal it!"

"Well, if I happen to have the means, I purchase it from the next available shop. If, on the other hand, I do not have the means to do so on a certain day, I roam the shops until I find a favourable opportunity to steal."

"But there are CCTV cameras all over the place."

"Never mind the cameras! In several instances, I am able not only to outwit the cameras but also the security at the exit. Well, that is not always the case, otherwise you wouldn't be interviewing me in prison today."

"What happens on the days that you are neither able to buy nor steal alcohol?"

"In that case, I head for the local hospital!"

"For the hospital? What has the hospital got to do with your search for alcohol?"

"There are disinfectants hanging about in the corridors of the hospitals!"

"What are you driving at?"

"Well, as you know, hospital disinfectants contain alcohol! I just look for a favourable moment when no one is watching, remove them and hide them in my coat. Back home I dilute it in water and use it as a substitute for alcohol."

"That can't be true! Disinfectants are not meant for human consumption!"

"Alcohol is alcohol, doc!" he concluded.

71) THE STATE'S UNMERCIFUL TREATMENET OF A POOR MOTHER

Once when I was on reception duty, I saw the name of a patient on the doctor's list who needed to be seen. A short while later, the name vanished from the screen. Not long later, I got this message from the reception nurse:

"You no longer need to see her. She was sent to prison for failure to pay a £300 council tax bill. Someone has paid it for her so she has been allowed to go back home."

It's not often that a matter is so easily resolved!

On one occasion when I was on reception duty on a female ward, the nurse on reception duty sent me this message through the internal mailing service:

"Could you please prescribe a short course of sleeping tablets for one of our recent arrivals? She is in prison for her inability to pay her council tax. Her partner is supposed to be looking after her children but she does not believe he is up to the task. She is in a very weepy state and unable to sleep. She has another four weeks to do – could you please help?"

I was really infuriated that the state should go to the extent of sending such a person to jail! The incident made me think of the words of my late mother who used to say: "I wish indeed, I was born rich. I would have been generous with my money – I cannot bear all the poverty one sees around us!"

I did not know the amount involved. Indeed, if I had heard of her case prior to her being sentenced, I would have gladly paid her council tax on her behalf, if only for the sake of her children. When I sit down to consider the manner in which some taxpayers' money is spent, I wonder why society is not able to spare a lady in this position the indignity of a jail sentence.

72) DEATH BY
DANGEROUS DRIVING

My daily drive to work takes me along a narrow road across a field. It links a major street to another major street that leads to the M1, one of the busiest motorways in the UK, about a mile away. There are no streets light along the field road.

It was around 6:30am on a January morning, and still quite dark. As I drove along that stretch of straight road for a distance of about one mile, I happened to be the only road user on the isolated road at this time of day – at least that was what I thought. My thoughts concentrated on the approximately 90-minute drive ahead of me, to a prison I was booked to work in, about 80 miles to the north of my place of residence.

I was driving at about 60mph, which was the speed limit on that stretch of road. Still there was no vehicular traffic evident, apart from me, either behind or in front of me.

Just about 300 yards before I was due to join the main road, suddenly my attention was drawn to a faint spot of red light a few metres ahead of me! Moments later the silhouette of a human being on a bike became evident on the road, in the same lane I was driving in – the road not having a cycle lane.

"My goodness!" I screamed to myself and pressed firmly on the brake pedal. I really thought I was going to crush the rider under my vehicle. Fortunately, my screeching front tyres managed to come to a halt just a few centimetres behind the rider.

My heart was beating hard and for a while I was frozen to the spot. Eventually I managed to calm my nerves to resume my journey.

The rider, who seemed unconcerned about what had happened behind him, continued his journey without even bothering to look back. Before long I caught up with him, crawling up to the traffic light connecting the field road to the main road.

He turned right and headed for the city, while I turned left and headed away from the city.

It was indeed a very lucky escape, not only for the cyclist, but for me as well. Having worked in the prison for some time now, I knew what would have been the outcome if I had failed to bring the car to a near halt and had hit and killed the cyclist! Though the cyclist's dimly illuminated tail light could hardly be considered a light, it would nevertheless have been considered to be adequate by the legal experts and I would most likely have been found guilty of failing to see his "well-illuminated" bicycle and causing his death – and death by dangerous driving would have been my charge.

All of a sudden, the prison doctor that I am would have experienced a role reversal!

Reader, I advise you to be extra careful on the road; circumstances beyond your control could easily lead to an accident that could result in death, which in turn could result in your being sent to prison on charges of death by dangerous driving.

Believe me, I have come across a few such cases during my prison work.

A case still fresh in my memory involved a truck driver from eastern Europe who ended up in jail on the above charges for causing an accident that led to death. He told me driving on the right-hand side of the road in the UK, contrary to the left-hand side that he was used to in his native country, caused him to fail to notice another driver, which set off the chain of events that resulted in motorway collisions involving several vehicles, with the subsequent loss of a few lives.

Then there was the case of young man in his mid-20s who, in his youthful exuberance, engaged in a car chase with his friend. In the event he drove into the rear of his friend's car, which resulted in him losing control of his vehicle, swerving to the other side of the road and colliding with an oncoming vehicle, killing its driver on the spot. His friend on his part suffered a broken spine leading to complete paralysis from the waist down.

At the time of our meeting he had just begun a six-year prison term for death by dangerous driving.

He was not a typical prisoner and appeared more enlightened than the average prisoner of his age. That was indeed the reason I wanted to find out more about him.

"Have you learnt your lesson for life?"

"Indeed, I have, doc. I realise how stupid I have been. But unfortunately, that is too late. My actions have resulted in someone losing his life, and the other being paralysed for life!"

73) MAKE SURE YOU ARE NOT CAUGHT!

B e warned if you have been disqualified from driving; any attempt to drive during the period of your disqualification could land you in prison – never mind if you offer to pay a heavy fine to prevent spending some days behind bars. (You might have the good fortune to be faced by a generous judge, but there is no guarantee you will!) Driving while disqualified is not only a jail sentence, but is likely to result in an extension of your ban.

There was the case of a noble-looking middle-aged man who came to prison. According to him the company he was working for had won a lucrative contract. The staff were invited to a party to celebrate the occasion and, after he drank a good deal of alcohol, he chose to drive home. He should have known better and left his vehicle at home and made use of a taxi.

His erratic style of driving caught the attention of an unmarked police patrol car and he was stopped. In the event it emerged that he was already disqualified from driving.

According to him, he earnestly pleaded with the judge to spare him a custodial sentence in exchange for a heavy fine – but the judge did not budge and sentenced him to several weeks in jail.

Then there's the case of a young student with well-to-do parents – at least that is what he made me to believe. He was disqualified from driving for persistently speeding with the Mercedes his parents had bought for him. When he was caught again breaking the speed limit after being disqualified, the judge did not heed his plea for clemency and sentenced him to a few weeks in prison. At the time of our meeting he was very distraught – having missed an important examination. For a while he had to spend his time with hardened criminals instead of aspiring academics within the walls of his university.

There was also the case of a young man, self-employed, who said he was dependent on his vehicle to run his business, without which he could not feed his family.

Well, he told me he was caught just at the time when his ban was about to be lifted. So apart from having to spend some time in prison, he had more days added to his ban.

74) "MARRIED TO A WITCH"

Usually the doctor on reception duty sits in a different office from that of the nurse on reception duty. On some occasions, due to computer breakdown, and due to a shortage of offices in the reception lounge, the reception doctor may find himself in the same office as the reception nurse. He will then have the opportunity to follow the healthcare reception screening process.

It involves standard questions requesting short answers, involving: ethnicity, marital status, recent admission to hospital, medical condition, etc.

One particular aspect of a reception screening interview that I witnessed is still embedded in my memory:

"What is your marital status?" the nurse inquired routinely.

"Pardon?"

"Marital status, please?"

"Not sure."

"Married?"

"Not sure."

"Divorced?"

"No!"

"Separated?"

"No!"

"What then?"

"I don't know how to put it!"

"What do you mean?"

"Well, I am married – married to a witch!"

"Indeed?"

"How else should I describe her? She screwed me up. I caught her red-handed in bed with someone else. She then decided to screw me up. In the end the jury believed her. That's how I was handed my seven-year sentence!"

75) "ME, NO ENGLISH; ME NO ENGLISH!"

When I worked in a London prison around 2010 quite a good number of the inmates I dealt with when I was on reception duty were eastern Europeans, from the countries that had recently joined the EU and whose citizens had gained the right to stay and work in the UK. Hardly had some entered the UK than they engaged in various criminal activities – theft, shoplifting, burglary, etc.

On one occasion when I was on duty, an inmate who was on my clinic list, on being asked the reason for wanting to see the doctor, began to gesticulate and utter the words:

"Me, no English; me no English!"

"If 'me no English; me no English', how did you manage to commit your crime?" the nurse serving as chaperone burst out.

"Does one need to understand English to pick pocket in the train?!" I inquired.

"Of course not; but it is really frustrating! It appears some of them just travel all the way from eastern Europe – Romania and Bulgaria especially – with the sole aim of pick-pocketing in the train or on the streets."

As I said above, this is a phenomenon that was observed in 2010. I stopped working in the London prison concerned in 2011. Whether the problem still persists at the time of writing these lines in 2016, is not clear to me.

76) PRISONER "MR ASSERTIVE"

O nce as I worked in a prison, I was asked to see an inmate in order to prescribe an alternative medication for his regular medication, which was temporarily unavailable on the market due to manufacturing problems. The name of the patient did not ring a bell in my ears. After presenting him with a few possible alternatives, we eventually agreed on a particular one. I booked him for a review four weeks later.

"The alternative medication you prescribed is working", he began after the initial exchange of greetings, "but not working very well." He continued: "I would be happy if you would revert to the original one. Indeed it was working wonders."

"Well", I said, "give me a moment while I check with Pharmacy."

Moments later I was dialling the prison pharmacy.

"Sorry", I was told, "the medication in question is still not available on the market!"

I passed the message on to the patient.

"That is bad, just too bad!" he said. "Is there anything you can do to influence the situation?"

"Unfortunately, I cannot. My duty is to prescribe. Pharmacy's duty is to dispense. When there is a nationwide manufacturer problem, there is little else one can do!"

"Bad, very bad", he shook his head, then suggested: "Okay, then I suggest you increase the dosage of the alternative."

"I started you on quite a high dose to start with", I explained, "in view of the fact that you were already on a high dose of the other one – so it should be enough for now."

"But I am not on the maximum dose", he objected. "I spoke with one of the nurses on the matter. I was told it could be increased to three tablets three times daily, instead of the current dose of two tablets three times daily."

"Which nurse did you speak to?" I asked.

"She was wearing a deep pink dress, has blonde hair, quite attractive!"

I realised at once who he meant – the lead nurse. Had he gone to the point of speaking to the lead nurse on the matter? And had she in turn made that suggestion?

I could have insisted on my own judgment, but decided to give him the benefit of the doubt and increased the dosage to three capsules three times daily – still short of the maximum dose permitted, however.

"Okay", I said, "I have increased your prescription to three capsules to be taken three times daily; I will see you again in four weeks' time to review this."

"Thanks, doc", he said, "but still do check with Pharmacy concerning the availability of the original medication."

"I will do so. You can also keep on checking with the dispensing nurses. They can check from Pharmacy on your behalf. The moment they are available again from the market, you can apply to see me to put you back on it."

As he left the room, I began to ponder over him – he seemed to be quite assertive in his behaviour. Not long after he had left the doctor's room, one of our Pharmacy assistants entered my room.

"I want the prescription of Prisoner X", she said. "You saw him not long ago. The prescription has appeared on the system. I need the chart to be able to dispense."

Usually, I keep all the prescription sheets till the end of the session before handing them in bulk to Pharmacy. The fact that the assistant was in a hurry for the sheet of that particular prisoner appeared strange to me.

Hardly had the assistant left the consulting room than I received a call from the pharmacist herself inquiring whether the assistant had been there to pick up the prescription sheet.

The assertive behaviour displayed by the prisoner during the consultation, coupled with the fact that both nursing and pharmacy staff seemed to pay particular attention to his needs, aroused a sense of curiosity in me. What type of inmate was he? Why was he in prison?

Though, up to that point in my prison work, it was not my habit so to do so, on this particular occasion I decided to Google his name, which sounded not typically English, to find out about him.

I had hardly begun to type in his name, than the search engine threw out numerous entries concerning his case, which made headline news in the UK in the 80s. He had been convicted in 1986 of the murder of his adoptive parents, adoptive sister and her six-year-old twin sons. Initially, it was thought his adoptive sister, who at that time had mental health issues (she had been diagnosed with schizophrenia) had committed the crime, that she had first murdered her adoptive parents plus her twin sons before turning the gun on herself. Indeed for several weeks after the murders the police and media believed she was the killer. The turning point in the matter came when the convict implicated himself during a conversation with his ex-girlfriend.

In the end the prosecution argued successfully that, after carrying out the murders to secure a large inheritance, the accused placed the gun in his 28-year-old sister's hands to make it look like a murder–suicide. He was eventually sentenced to life, to serve 25 years. Based on the original sentence he should be back in the community by now. My information is that he has been told he would never be released.

77) LEARNING SESSIONS FOR THE LEARNED

I n some instances my consultations have turned into learning sessions for myself.

I had one such "learning session" in a female prison. It involved a female inmate who not very long prior to her incarceration, had undergone gender change – from male to female.

What I was not aware of was that over the next several months after such a procedure, there was the need for the patient to place a dilating device into the newly created female organ to prevent it from collapsing. The patient informed me the plastic surgeons had asked her to carry out three self-dilatation sessions per day, with each session lasting an hour.

The reason for the consultation was that, based on the instructions she had received from the plastic surgeon, a dilatation device of a larger size than the one she had was due about the time of her arrest.

She wanted to find out if healthcare could help her acquire the device of the requisite size.

Not only was the issue unchartered territory for me, the female nurse chaperoning me was also at a loss as to how to assist her!

In the end, I delegated the matter to my assistant, asking her to contact healthcare administration to find a way out. Later on during the day, she reported back to me.

"Doc, Admin gave me some numbers to call for advice on the matter. So far, no one seems to have an idea as to how to assist the lady. I will keep on trying though. I will record the outcome in her notes so do check next time you are around – in case you are interested in the outcome."

I did not return to that prison for a while. I would indeed have wished to follow up on the matter, had her name not slipped my memory at the time of my return.

78) THE PRISONER WITH A LOST IDENTITY

A few weeks prior to her release from prison, a prisoner approached me to issue a sick note for her to enable her to claim disability allowance on her release. "That is not possible", I said. "The moment you step out of prison, we are no longer in charge so we cannot issue such a note. You will need to contact a GP in the community instead for such a note."

"That's easier said than done!" she said.

"What do you mean by that?"

"I need an ID to register, something I do not have."

"Where is your ID?"

"It's missing."

"Well, you can apply for one."

"Easier said than done", she said again.

"Why?"

"I don't have a birth certificate."

"Why not?"

"It's missing."

"How did you lose both of these important documents?"

"This is what happened", she explained. "At the time of my arrest, I had no documents on me. The police established my identity by cross-checking my fingerprints with the data they were keeping in the national offenders' register. In the end I was sent to prison without being allowed to go home to collect my identity papers. I live in a rented property. At the time of my arrest there was money in my account to pay my rent for a few months. Well, in the course of time that money was exhausted. After I had defaulted on the rent payment for a while, the landlord sought and obtained a removal or clearance order from the courts. Eventually the landlord cleared my room of everything, including my identity papers – birth certificate, driving licence, passport. So now I have no identity!"

"You must speak to social services", I advised. "There must be a way out."

"I am doing my best", she said. "They don't seem to care less though. Today for example, I had a video link appointment with my probation officer. She just cancelled the appointment at the last minute."

"I am sure there will be a way out for you", I said. "Everyone knows you need a form of ID to find your way out in the free world."

79) EIGHT MONTHS FOR TWO PIECES OF ICE!

Sometimes when I interact with relatively young inmates, those aged around 20 years and below, I try to play the "father role" in an attempt to impact in a positive way on their lives. That is particularly the case when I realise from conversations with the inmates that there is a potential for correction. (I do not want to go into details to state exactly how I am able to come to that conclusion.)

This was the case with a pleasant 19-year-old inmate in a female prison.

"You should be going to college instead of spending time in prison, young lady!" I began.

"I am aware of that, doc. The thought of being the black sheep of my family really saddens me!"

"You have brothers and sisters?"

"I have a brother. Both of us were adopted by our loving parents. Unfortunately, I have let the family down through my addiction to alcohol!"

"It's not too late to turn over a new leaf!"

"I will do my best. I will be released soon on licence. I hope my family will help me keep to the conditions of my release."

"What are the conditions?"

"During the time of my licence I am barred from entering any grocery shop in our little town!"

"That is hard!"

"Well, I will have to get my parents and brother to do my shopping for me!"

"Why did they impose that restriction?"

"Well, it is in response to the offence that brought me to jail!"

"What happened?"

"One day, I was quite drunk – but still wanted more drink. I did not have money on me so I went to one of the grocery stores. I called the attention of one of the shop attendants when I got to the drinks section and asked: 'Give me this, give me this, give me that!' After a while they were fed up with me, so they called the police. Because I was on licence for a previous offence, I was sent back to jail!" She shook her head. "The system is not working, doc! Instead of solving the root cause, they are dealing only with the symptoms!" She went on: "Doc, can you imagine it! There is a lady here who has been sent to prison to serve the remaining eight months of her licence just for stealing two pieces of ice cream. Eight months for two pieces of ice cream, doc! She did not steal to sell. She was just hungry and needed something to eat!"

80) AN 88-YEAR-OLD'S DESPERATE STRUGGLE TO FULFIL PAROLE REQUIREMENTS

Then there was the 88-year-old inmate sentenced on sex-related offences.

As might be expected of someone of his age, he displayed various age-related disabilities; he was not only impaired in his vision, he was not quite strong on his legs, leading him to resort to a wheelchair for mobilisation.

He told me during one consultation that in order for him to be considered for parole, he needed to take part in a course designed especially for sex offenders.

"How do they expect someone of my age with my impairment of vision, to sit in a classroom not only to listen, but also take notes from a screen positioned several feet ahead of me?"

"Well, you have to convince the probation authorities to make an exception for you. Maybe you could just go and then listen, without the need to write anything."

"Even that is a problem, doc. Now my good friend, let's be realistic. How on earth do they expect a person of my age to be able not only to listen to such a lecture, but also to keep the stuff in my mind to reproduce in a test situation?"

"Well, you've got to find a way to convince the parole board to either grant you an exemption or modify the training to suit your age."

"Well, I hope they understand, otherwise I have no choice but to stay here to the bitter end – in which case, we shall be seeing each other quite often."

"Well, I am an agency doctor, not under contract of the healthcare. They can at any time decide not to book me for further sessions. On my part, too, I can decide at any time to stop this job."

"Well, then we'll keep on seeing each other as long as the Man Upstairs permits it!" And he pointed heavenwards.

"That's exactly so", I smiled.

In the course of time, this frail, elderly inmate, who was among one of the frequent visitors to the healthcare department, became one of my favourite patients.

During one consultation, he turned to me and began:

"Do you want to learn something from a traveller's child?"

"Go ahead, please."

"Well, you are a doctor; did you know that the grease from whole cooked geese has medicinal qualities?"

"No idea!"

"My grandmother used it to treat us when we were children. Whenever she prepared a whole goose for the family, she collected the grease and put it aside. When one of us had a cough from the flu or whatever cause, she used it as topical ointment, applying it to the chest and back of the patient. And it did indeed relieve the symptoms! Besides that, she also used it to treat various skin conditions – eczema, nappy rash as well as various skin infections."

During one meeting I had with him shortly before one Christmas, he asked me unexpectedly:

"Has your wife already bought a turkey or goose for the occasion?"

"I think she has."

"Well, she might try my dear grandmother's way of preparing the bird."

"Indeed, I hope I am able to remember all you have told me."

"Well, before roasting the Christmas turkey, grandma would dip it in white wine or pure Jamaican rum for a while so as to soften the meat before finally roasting it. That way of treating it bequeathed the meat a special taste!"

"What else has your 88-year-old memory bank have in store for me?"
"I will let you know the next time we meet."

81) LEGAL WRANGLING AROUND THE UNBORN CHILD

Then there was the case of a 26-year-old woman in the final days of her pregnancy, sentenced to five years for ABH and GBH. She would not be released before 2017.

With her unborn baby due in a few days, legal wrangling was ongoing in regard to the future of the unborn baby. At the time of the consultation she was still awaiting the court's decision. As might be expected, she was very distraught.

Though the baby's father was visiting his partner in prison, he had been found by social services as not demonstrating an interest in and responsibility for raising a child – a negative assessment.

Next in line was the maternal grandmother who was already caring for her three-year-old child; without parental responsibility, the responsibility still rested in the hands of the mother in prison.

The court still had to decide on both cases.

When I returned to work in the same prison, out of curiosity I checked on her case.

What she had feared had come to pass – the baby had been put into foster care. She was upset and crying most of the time. The staff were doing their best to help her to encourage her – urging her to talk to friends/nurses/officers.

82) FATHER BEARING THE BRUNT OF SON'S MISCHIEF

I still remember the conversation I had with a 28-year-old male inmate. He began by revealing that he first came into conflict with the law when he was just ten years old.

"What happened?"

"Shoplifting!"

"Shoplifting what?"

"Chocolate; it was really tempting. I had no money on me so I just snatched it! Well, I was confronted by the shop's security! They took my name and address but let me walk free when I mentioned my age. I thought that was the end of the matter. But no! Later on in the day, I was at home with my parents when we heard the doorbell ringing. Not suspecting anything, my mother went to open it. To her surprise, she was confronted by two police officers!"

"'What's the matter?' my mother asked.

"'We have come to arrest Mr So-and So!' they stated emphatically.

"'Why?' my mother inquired, flabbergasted.

"'We have come to arrest him for shoplifting.'

"'You can't be serious – he has not been out the whole day!'

"Ignoring my mother, they informed my father that he was under arrest for shoplifting and set about handcuffing him. What they were not aware of was that my father had chosen to name his first son exactly after himself. What they were not aware of also was that the crime had been committed by me and not my father. Since no one had asked me anything up to that moment, I had chosen to keep quiet.

"Realising the seriousness of the situation, my mother turned to me: 'You have been out playing. Did you do that?' Shivering all over my body, I had no choice but to admit the offence!"

"That's an incredible story!" I said.

"Well, I have been a prolific offender since then! I seem to be unaware of my parameters or limits. I easily lose my temper. The situation is worsened by alcohol. In such situations, I easily get myself involved in fights. I'm not bragging, but I usually win most of my fights! One would think that once my victim is on the ground and at my mercy I would cease from inflicting further harm on him. That however is my problem. I keep on inflicting even more serious harm to him. I am an IPP [one being held under an Indefinite Public Protection Order]. So long as I am unable to get over that, it's unlikely I'll be released any time soon!"

83) THERE IS NO ART TO FIND THE MIND'S CONSTRUCTION IN THE FACE

"There's no art
To find the mind's construction in the face.
He was a gentleman on whom I built
An absolute trust."
From Shakespeare's *Macbeth*

Though the crime that brought an individual to prison may be mentioned in his or her medical records, they are usually touched upon in summary.

It is superfluous to mention here that in the age of the internet, one can hardly hide details of a crime, especially when it involves a high profile, headline-grabbing case. Indeed whoever is desirous of finding out further details about such matters can easily search the internet for the relevant information.

Hardly has one started typing the name of the individual involved into a search engine than, lo and behold, one is confronted with the details. The information spewed out might well send cold chills down the spine of the inquirer.

How come the genteel, the innocent-looking, soft-spoken individual who comes across as friendly and polite throughout our meeting conceals the appalling evil deed linked to his/her name? What on earth could have driven such an individual to commit despicable crimes?

Much as our calling as healthcare professionals demands emotional distance in our dealing with our patients, in not a few instances I have, after such experiences, if even for a short while, struggled to keep my emotions under control. An instance is the case of a young man in his mid-20s who once came for treatment for a distortion to his ankle while playing football. In the course of his history-taking he mentioned that he had fractured the same ankle a few years before whilst serving in the Royal Army.

"From a soldier in the Royal Army to a prison inmate!" I exclaimed. "What happened?" I inquired.

He merely shrugged his shoulders, choosing to keep his silence.

Realising he was not comfortable speaking about what had led him to prison, I decided not to dwell on the matter any further and instead concentrated on his medical condition.

Occasionally, I do ask some of my patients at the end of the consultation about their expected release date. That was the case with this particular patient as well.

"The earliest I can be considered for parole will be 2046", he revealed.

"Thirty-one years from now!" I exclaimed, taken somewhat aback by the exceptionally long sentence.

"Yes, you heard me right", he nodded.

"That's really a very long time", I said. "It's indeed one of the longest jail terms I have come across in my work as a prison doctor."

"Well, that's my lot!" he smiled ruefully and said, "Bye for now, doc." With that he walked out of the room.

His decision not to talk about his crime coupled with the fact of his long prison sentence aroused my curiosity, which in turn prompted me to Google his name as soon as he had left the room. Yet I really wish now I had not taken that step! Throughout the rest of the day and several days thereafter his case haunted me!

As I found out, he was sentenced for the most horrendous crime imaginable – rape and the subsequent murder of a teenage girlfriend of his second cousin! What made the crime even more gruesome was the fact that the victim was heavily pregnant. According to the report, she was expecting her baby daughter a few days prior to becoming the victim of the ghastly crime. Not only did the perpetrator of the crime stab the expectant mother to death, he also appallingly did the same to the unborn baby she was carrying.

As if this catalogue of horrific events were not enough, he then set fire to the crime scene in an effort to cover up his monstrous deeds.

One asks how such an innocent-looking gentleman can be human at one instance and the personification of evil at the next. I am still wondering about this Jekyll and Hyde phenomenon.

Though my profession requires that I treat everyone equally, I knew it would require a huge effort on my part to do so in such cases. I only wish I had been spared the need to treat him again. But I wasn't. Several weeks after our first meeting, I reported to work only to find his name on my clinic list for the day!

Well, how could I deny him treatment? I had to struggle throughout the consultation to maintain an emotional distance towards him.

Even as I write, I still do wonder how that innocent-looking young man could be associated with a crime one might associate only with a monster.

84) BETTER HEALTHY IN PRISON THAN DEAD IN THE COMMUNITY

The following conversation ensued between myself and a 63-year-old inmate.

"Doc, I have received bad news", he announced.

"What is it about?"

"A good friend of mine has died of prostate cancer in the community."

"That's really sad. How old was he?"

"Just about my age. He did not have the time to go for a check-up. When he finally decided to go to the doctor due to feeling unwell, it took quite a while before he got an appointment. In the end his cancer was diagnosed at an advanced stage."

"Really?"

"Well, that's the reason why I'm happy to be in prison! At least over here I enjoy good healthcare! You know from my records that I have also had surgery for prostate cancer. If I had been at home, I might have suffered a similar fate as my friend. Thanks to the good healthcare in this prison, my case was detected early. At that time you had not started working here. I described my symptoms to a female doctor who used to work here. She initiated all the necessary tests. Eventually, my cancer was detected at quite an early stage. I have in the meantime had surgery and all the necessary post-surgical treatment. Now as you can see I'm in quite good health."

PART FOUR
A PAUSE FOR REFLECTIONS

85) A FORMER EXECUTION SITE AND THE BLOOMING FLOWERS

As I was being escorted from the gates of a prison I had been sent to by my agency to work for the first time, my attention was drawn to a beautiful set of flowers growing in an open yard, about 10 yards by 10 yards in dimension. It was spring and the flowers were in bloom. I expressed my admiration for the wonderful shades of colours of the flowers in full blossom there – rich purple and crimson, pure white, delicate lilac, pale yellow, you name them!

"Do you want to know what role that plot of land served in former times?" my guide asked.

"Well, I am curious to know!"

"That happened to be the location of the prison gallows!"

"Indeed?"

"Yes, this is a Victorian age prison. In those days, hanging was part of the penal code."

"How times have changed!"

"Well, personally I sometimes wish capital punishment is re-introduced. Those were the days when prisons were real prisons and prisoners real prisoners. These days prisons have become like holiday resorts!"

The death sentence has been abolished in almost every European country – thank goodness, in my view.

The question that societies in which the death sentence has been abolished should ask themselves is – what type of rights should we grant offenders spared the death sentence after they themselves have taken the lives of others, in some cases through very gruesome and ghastly means, during their time in prison? Having deprived their victims of their right to life, should they be permitted unrestricted claims to existing human rights laws and conventions?

While not advocating that the perpetrators of heinous crimes that lead to the loss of lives of their victims should be deprived of the basic necessities of life – water, food, clothing and medical care, etc. – should society for example permit them unrestricted claims to human rights provisions?

For example, where an inmate convicted for taking someone else's life slips while exercising in the gym – whether genuinely or through suspicious circumstances and breaks a limb – should that individual have the right to claim monetary compensation for that injury?

86) MUCH ADO ABOUT NOTHING!

I n view of the energy and effort usually expended in handling inmates sent to prison, I submit that in order to reduce the pressures on our prisons, society should take a closer or second look at sentencing guidelines related to minor crimes requiring short sentences.

Readers will recall the case of the lady who spent only a night in prison! Apart from being a sheer waste of prison resources and taxpayers' money, what purpose does it serve to send someone to jail only to be released within a matter of a few weeks or even days? Do we for example need to sentence a mother who is solely responsible for the care of her children to four weeks in jail for an inability to pay council tax?

I submit that in future society should make it obligatory for those who set the rules and those who implement or execute them to spend a few days in prisons observing the day-to-day running of a prison in order to appreciate the implication of their actions.

Until this happens, I shall take this opportunity to give them a brief overview from the point of view of a prison doctor.

Points to consider:

- First the transport from the court to the prison.
- Next to consider is the time and energy spent screening prisoners on their arrival, both by prison officers and healthcare staff.

If they happen to be on medication, healthcare administration will devote time the next day contacting their respective surgeries for confirmation. The confirmation usually must be in writing, usually in the form of a fax. Some surgeries respond promptly and send the confirmation without delay. There are times though when such confirmations are delayed. I mentioned earlier that prisons work with community pharmacies. By the time the pharmacies send in the medication prescribed by the doctor, an inmate serving a short sentence may in fact be nearing the end of a short sentence. Even though the prescription issued for the inmate on such a short sentence might still be valid, the doctor is called upon to issue another prescription for so-called *to take outs* (TTOs) medication. TTOs are usually prescribed for seven days. They are meant to bridge the time gap between the individual's release from prison and the first opportunity for the individual to contact his/her community GP for prescription.

If only for such considerations, the author humbly submits that any sentence below three months should be suspended or turned into fines or whatever punishment society deems appropriate, short of an actual prison sentence.

87) PAY DAY FOR SEASONED CRIMINALS

One day when I was on my rounds on a hospital-like ward of a prison, the lead nurse pointed to a gentleman in his mid-30s walking along the corridor a few yards ahead of us.

"Do you remember a high-profile case involving the young girl who was kidnapped from a playground not long ago?" the lead nurse asked.

"Yes I do. It was said that the young girl was familiar with the perpetrator so she might not have suspected any sinister motives when she climbed into his vehicle."

"Well, he was convicted of the heinous crime."

"Indeed?!"

"Exactly. Not long after his arrival here, he was assaulted by another inmate in a revenge attack related to his offence. I understand he received a substantial monetary pay-out as compensation. The parents of the poor girl will surely be boiling with rage should they get to know about it!"

This raises the question whether society should permit such payments to such vile criminals?

I consider it an insult both to the memory of the departed and his/her family that the perpetrator of the crime should benefit from a sizable monetary compensation!

This individual takes someone else's life in a ghastly manner, a crime that in earlier times would with all certainty have carried the death penalty. Society has spared him that. Now the same society is lamenting infringements on *his rights*; not only that, the same society goes to the extent of awarding him a huge pay-out for the infringement of his human rights!!

Earlier in my narration, I referred to the solicitors' adverts and touched on the tendency of prisoners to seek compensation for any perceived infringement of their rights, no matter how whimsical these may be.

It is a fact that a considerable amount of money – taxpayers' money at that – is spent on compensation pay-outs in prison. I recently read the online edition of *The Daily Mail* of 2011 which reported that over a period of five years preceding the time of the publication, prisoners had been paid total compensation of £10m, that is an average of £2m annually.

I do not know who came up with the prison laws that have led to the above situation. Indeed, at the end of the day, it is the lawmakers who must account for the matter, for prisoners and the solicitors who represent them are just interpreting existing laws.

My question to the lawmakers therefore is – why should the taxpayer compensate a prisoner who is injured while exercising in the gym of a prison without any third party involvement?

If an ordinary law-abiding citizen should walk on the street, and slip and fall – if he/she does not have any private insurance, then that's the end of the matter. Why should the situation be different when it comes to prison inmates? Why should breakers of the law enjoy privileges not available to the law-abiding population?

In case of injuries sustained accidentally in jail, inmates should have rights to medical care; indeed, our common humanity dictates that we help any other human being who finds him or herself in such a situation. Medical care for an injured prison inmate, yes; monetary compensation, no!

To create a sense of fairness, and also for the sake of the victims of such horrible crimes and their relatives, I humbly submit that this state of affairs should be rectified without delay.

I humbly propose the following.

The prevailing sentencing guidelines for once capital crimes and other serious crimes should be supplemented with additional guidelines that will place restrictions on the perpetrators' ability to claim rights on the grounds of existing human rights laws.

Such restrictions on their rights could be laid down by an independent panel in a manner similar to the existing categorisation of prisoners into Cat A, B, C, D prisoners subject to review from time to time.

For example, an offender could be sentenced to life imprisonment with Cat A restriction on his/her human rights. Inmates placed on such a high restriction of their rights would be entitled only to very basic rights needed to exist. They would have no right to compensation on whatever grounds. Even should a breach warranting compensation be established during their sentence, the resulting pay-out should go to a charity instead of the individual involved.

88) JUDGEMENT DAY FOR THOSE ROBBED OF THEIR WILL-POWER

Having worked in the Prison Service for over a decade, during which time I have regularly had to deal with inmates addicted to various substances and who have been sentenced for drug-related offences – in the main relating to crimes committed with the goal of acquiring the means to purchase drugs – I have entertained doubts as to whether society's current approach to the complex issues of drug addiction is appropriate. We seem indeed inclined to treat the symptoms instead of the causes of the problem of drug addiction.

My view is that society should do all it can to prevent those who have never tried their hand at substances of addiction from doing so.

Parents, guardians, teachers, religious leaders, social workers, indeed all who by virtue of their position in society have an influence in the upbringing of children, should do all in their power to prevent our children from treading the path that could lead to drug addiction.

The saying also has it that prevention is better than cure. It is indisputable that no one is born a drug addict – although babies born to those addicted to drugs show withdrawal symptoms at birth; but that certainly cannot be classified as addiction in the real sense of the word.

Yes, let us make a concerted effort at prevention; prevention, prevention, should be our watchword, and prevention should be the main focus of our fight against drug abuse.

If, despite all measures to prevent an individual from becoming addicted to one or more substances of addiction – indeed, if after all appeals, education, warnings from parents, guardians, relatives, teachers, social workers, etc., aimed at preventing an individual from using substances of addiction – that individual nevertheless eventually becomes addicted to one or more of the substances of abuse, society, in my opinion, should at that point take a different approach from what pertains at the moment, which treats those who commit petty crime to fund their addiction as criminals and send them to jail. Instead of treating the addicts as criminals, we must consider them as sick or diseased individuals needing our help.

The *Merriam-Webster* online English dictionary defines illness as

1. a condition of being unhealthy in your body or mind;
2. a specific condition that prevents your body or mind from working normally.

See http://www.merriam-webster.com/dictionary/illness

A condition of being unhealthy in your body or mind, a condition that prevents your body or mind from working normally – that exactly is the state that a full-blown heroin, alcohol, cocaine addict finds himself or herself in.

Indeed, the moment an individual becomes addicted to any substance of addiction, that individual should be classified with the sick, not with those suffering from an acute medical condition such as appendicitis, which can be treated leaving the patient healed. No, a drug addict is not suffering from an acute condition but rather a chronic one, a condition that could persist indefinitely. In the same way that society generally has compassion for its sick and disabled, society should pity individuals addicted to drugs instead of criminalising them.

Those who do not see eye to eye with me in this argument may tell me outright that it is usually beyond one's control whether one is afflicted with a disease or not. "It was not my fault that I caught a chest infection", one might tell me. Again: "It was not within my power to prevent myself from developing an acute appendicitis." Yet a third person might make the following point, where a mishap might be the result of circumstances: "I was not responsible for the fault that developed in the bus I was travelling in, which in turn resulted in an accident which caused me to break a limb."

So, it is surely evident that one cannot compare these respective situations with that of a drug addict. The path that led to an individual's addiction began as a matter of choice. Indeed no one forced the addicts to try their hand at cocaine, heroin, alcohol, as the case may be, in the first place. Those who fall sick on the other hand did not look out for their diseases.

While I do not dispute this, we should not lose sight of the fact that in any of us the danger lurks of giving way to temptation, for none of us is surely immune from temptation, and in most cases prone to mistakes, wrong choices, wrong decisions that could lead us to situations that we would never have wished for ourselves. For example, one failure to resist the inborn weakness of the flesh, could lead us to a reckless sexual encounter with a stranger, which in turn could lead us to contract HIV.

Agreed, an individual can make a mistake by trying his or her hand on a substance of addiction, which in turn may lead to his or her entrapment in the powerful claws of the monster called Addiction! In such a situation, does society have to inflict more suffering by sending the individual to jail instead of helping the wretched fellow out of the mess? It's like a boxer who has floored his/her opponent in the ring, neglecting the plea of the referee as well as the opponent struggling to get up and inflicting even more suffering!

Indeed the bare truth is that the moment an individual becomes addicted to any of the substances of addiction, that individual has surrendered his/her willpower to the substance in question and can no longer be held responsible for their actions. To put it bluntly, that individual is in captivity, held against his or her will by the monster drug concerned.

We may compare the situation to that of the manager of a bank who is held at gun point by robbers demanding that he empties the bank safe and fills the empty bags they are carrying with bank notes. Much as the law will not punish such an individual for doing the bidding of the robbers, in the same way, I humbly submit, society should find a different approach to addicts committing petty crimes like shoplifting to fund their addiction.

Readers, I have dealt with numerous cases of persons addicted to drugs during my work in prison. They have indeed literally lost control – they are no longer in charge of their mind or their activities. They are individuals whose minds are no longer working normally, whose willpower has been compromised and surrendered to the power of drugs. They will do whatever it takes to obtain the means to satisfy their cravings – sell their bodies, their precious gold, silver, diamonds, indeed any possession of value, whatever it takes to satisfy their craving for the addicted substance in question.

It is not only a matter of their minds; their bodies having become used to the substance involved will begin literally to "rebel" against them when deprived of the substance involved over a period, leading to physical discomfort in the form of withdrawal symptoms.

I shall refer to the case of a woman in her mid-20s I saw at the reception clinic in February 2016 as an example. She was sent to prison charged with stealing a lady's handbag, shorts and underwear to the value of £635. What led this decent and innocent-looking young woman with quite good looks into such a situation? Simply put – her addiction to drugs, indeed her enslavement to drugs!

Besides being on methadone-substitution therapy, receiving 80mg of the opiate substitution medication daily, she was also reported to be injecting £150 worth of heroin into her bloodstream daily. In addition to this, she also admitted to consuming £200 worth of cocaine, taking "18 blue tablets" of diazepam, corresponding to 180mg, daily as well as drinking as much Cherry and Special Brew as she could get hold of from morning till bedtime.

"How is your body coping with the daily intake of such a substantial amount of these 'poisonous chemicals'?" I inquired, deeply saddened by her case. "Doc", she replied, "I have the impression my body will shut down one of these days, and that will be that!"

Dear reader, what do you make of such an individual who shoplifts to fund her addiction? A criminal needing to be put behind bars, or a sick individual desperately in need of treatment?

In my view – you may disagree with me – such a person is best helped in a rehabilitation institute or home, not in a prison.

She is indeed sick, a miserable wretch, who has lost her willpower to the substances she is addicted to. I am not implying that I applaud her for going about shoplifting – I am simply saying that sending her to jail in the hope of ridding society of the menace of the drug problem is a woefully inadequate approach to the complex problem of drug addiction. Those who favour such an approach might, unlike the writer of these lines, not have had a real "battlefield" confrontation with the problem. They would otherwise appreciate how futile the present approach of sending those who commit petty crimes to fund their addiction to prison really is. Not only does it amount to a deplorable waste of time, of resources, and working time of the staff involved; in the end it boils down to fighting only the *symptoms*, day in and day out, without tackling the real root *cause* of the complex problem.

I am aware that what I consider an enlightened approach is unlikely to gain majority approval. Surely no one, including myself, wants to be a victim of crime, however minor. Water however flows in the direction of least resistance. In the same vein, politicians and lawmakers have a tendency to ride on the waves of public opinion – if only for their own political survival. Capitalising on the trend in society that favours tough action against crime, our policy makers are making it absolutely clear to all and sundry that "those who commit crime should be arrested, tried, and punished to deter others from emulating their examples!"

But will this tough talk ever prevent a heroin or alcohol addict whose body is already displaying unpleasant withdrawal symptoms for lack of heroin or alcohol as the case may be from taking every possible step, including shoplifting, burglary, petty crime, etc., to get at the funds needed to purchase the substance in question? As I mentioned earlier, such individuals are no longer in charge of their own actions.

How then should society deal with the problem of drug addiction? Indeed, what should society do with drug addicts who keep on committing crime to fund their addiction? Indeed, how does society help these individuals caught in the vicious cycle – crime, imprisonment, release, crime, imprisonment, release, and then yet more crime – to break the awful cycle?!

I certainly do not claim to have answers to all the complex issues revolving around the drug problem. I do however want to humbly present the following proposals for society's consideration.

Instead of sending drug addicts who commit crime to fund their addiction to prison, we should instead consider setting up what I will describe as community drug villages or resettlement centres where addicts can be sent for treatment. Some might say such facilities already exist. I am not denying the fact that some rehabilitation centres do indeed exist. What is new in my proposal is the complete abolishment of the practice whereby individuals who commit petty crime to fund their addiction are sent to prison, to clog up the criminal justice system. Instead, after their arrest by the police, a judge should sentence them to spend time for appropriate treatment at the rehabilitation centre instead of serving a punishment sentence in prison. This would call for the setting up of additional centres to supplement existing ones. Such centres should not be subjected to the strict security protocol of a typical prison. Measures should however be put in place to prevent residents from escaping back into the mainstream of society – until such time that they are considered healed.

A rehabilitation centre could indeed be operated along the lines of an open prison, with the exception that those sent there would not be permitted back into mainstream society until they are deemed by a panel of independent members of the criminal justice system to have overcome their addiction.

89) "WE ARE THE IMPRISONER OF EUROPE!"

"We have to reduce the number of people in prison, we just have to... We are the imprisoner of Europe" – Frances Crook, chief executive of the Howard League for Penal Reform, *BBC News Online*: 25 February 2016.

I agree completely with the above statement. Has this situation come about because the sentencing guidelines are so rigid, indeed to the extent of not being flexible for adjustment as should be dictated by common sense? Or does a "I will show you how power lies" attitude on the part of some magistrates and judges prevent a common sense interpretation of the guidelines?

During my work as a prison doctor, I have come across various cases where people have been sent to jail for minor offences. In such situations, I am inclined to ask the question: "What was the rationale behind the sentence? Is it punishment; is it retribution; is it a deliberate waste of the taxpayers' money, or what?" Should society, for example, send a mother of four not able to pay her council tax to prison?

I referred earlier in my narration to the case of a lady who was sent back to prison for breach of her probation licence by dint of her stealing two pieces of ice cream! Couldn't society have come up with a better and more lenient way of treating the "crime"?

As far as I am concerned, any sentence that does not exceed a period of 12 weeks should not be custodial.

Under existing regulations, prisoners are usually released on licence after serving half of their prison term. Thus a person sentenced to six weeks will usually be released on licence after serving three weeks.

What is sentencing someone to spend three weeks in a UK jail intended to achieve – the punishment of the offender?

Let's weigh the 'perceived' punishment meted out to the lawbreaker against the cost to the state – free food, free medical care, free accommodation, not to mention the salaries of prison officers and other ancillary staff.

In my view the state is better served by imposing non-custodial sentences that will require them to engage in various activities – working in factories, shops, etc., caring for the elderly and the handicapped, performing community-related jobs, and suchlike.

I also have in mind individuals jailed for crimes committed in a state of obvious mental and emotional distress. Whilst admitting the fact that arson is a serious crime, should society send an individual to prison who in an attempt to commit suicide sets fire to his/her apartment?

Some will probably take the view that the individual deserves to be punished for endangering the lives of others. In my view society needs to help that individual out of his/her despairing situation rather than seek to punish him/her. I have in mind the case of a 21-year-old inmate who went on to hang herself in the prison where she was being held on arson charges resulting from her previous attempt to end her life by setting fire to her apartment. Had society sought to help her out of her desperate situation instead of sending her to jail, the outcome might have been different.

90) FREE BOARDING, FREE LODGING

In conclusion, my advice to every individual living in the UK – it may apply to other western European countries too – is to do whatever is in your power to prevent people becoming victims of crime; for the worst that can happen to the perpetrator of a crime of which you are a victim is for him/her to land in a UK jail – which as I pointed out at very beginning of this narrative is better described as a "holiday camp" than a jail.

In some sense it is even better than a holiday camp – for in a holiday camp, one has to pay for one's boarding and lodging; in a UK prison-turned-holiday-camp, one gets everything for free!

EPILOGUE: PRISON REFORM
WITH SOME SHORTFALLS

O n 18th May 2016, just as I was in the process of completing my
narrative, the Government, in a policy statement, also known as
the Queen's Speech by virtue of the fact that it is delivered by the Queen
on behalf of the Prime Minister, outlined wide-ranging measures aimed
at reform of the UK prison system.

At the heart of the reform package is rehabilitation. Subsequently,
there are plans to invest heavily in rehabilitative programmes.

Also as part of the reform, prisoners fulfilling certain criteria would
be released with tags to work in the community during the week and
return to prison at weekends.

Critics of the proposed changes point to the fact, among other things,
that the measures fail to tackle the central issue of prison population size.
Prisons have become dangerously overcrowded and understaffed, with
rising levels of violence and drug abuse, they point out.

I am inclined to side with the critics in the matter. There is indeed
the need to bring down the UK prison population which, according to
recent figures, is the third largest among 50 European countries, behind
only Russia and Turkey.

As a way of achieving a reduction in the prison population, policy
makers, in my view, need to take a second look at the existing sentencing
guidelines.

In a high profile case that recently made international news headlines,
a world renowned football star was sentenced to 21 months in prison
in Spain on tax-evasion charges. The individual involved, however,

escaped actually going to prison, the reason being that under the Spanish system, prison terms of under two years for individuals without a prior conviction can be served under probation.

Introducing a similar system in the UK with a reduced threshold of even 12 months could lead to a substantial decrease in the prison population.

Earlier on I raised the issue of drug addicts sent to jail for petty crimes related to their addiction. A reform of the existing sentencing guidelines that allows for such individuals to be sentenced to drug rehabilitation homes, instead of to prisons, could also lead to a considerable reduction in the prison population.

Notwithstanding the aforementioned critique, the proposed reform with its emphasis on rehabilitation, no doubt is a step in the right direction. It is hoped it achieves its primary objective of reducing reoffending, cutting crime and improving public safety.

"No longer will prisons be warehouses for criminals; they will now be places where lives are changed", to quote a line from the statement.

On that optimistic note, I do hereby rest my case!

CPSIA information can be obtained
at www.ICGtesting.com
Printed in the USA
LVOW13s1652291216

519136LV00010B/943/P